Magical Meditations

Guided Imagery for the Pagan Path

Yasmine Galenorn

THE CROSSING PRESS
Berkeley / Toronto

Text copyright © 2003 by Yasmine Galenorn

All rights reserved. No part of this book may be reproduced in any form, except brief excerpts for the purpose of review, without written permission of the publisher.

The Crossing Press
www.crossingpress.com

A division of Ten Speed Press
P.O. Box 7123
Berkeley, California 94707
www.tenspeed.com

Originally published in 1997 under the title *Trancing the Witch's Wheel*.

Library of Congress Cataloging-in-Publication Data on file with the publisher.
ISBN 1-58091-155-2

Cover design by Carole Goodman
Text design by Jeff Brandenburg/Image-Comp.com

First printing this edition, 2003
Printed in Canada

1 2 3 4 5 6 7 8 9 10 — 08 07 06 05 04 03

Dedication:

To my favorite authors:

Even though I never met you, I've learned so much from your books
and your poetry: Ray Bradbury, Daphne du Maurier, Richard Adams,
Charlotte Brontë, Amy Tan, Annie Dillard, W. B. Yeats, George
Meredith, Oscar Wilde, Henrik Ibsen, Diane Mott Davidson, J. A. Jance,
George Eliot, James Herriot, J.R.R. Tolkien, Michael Crichton,
Kenneth Grahame, Robert Frost, Langston Hughes, and A. A. Milne.

What can I say but, thank you all?

In the parched path
   I have seen the good lizard
   (one drop of crocodile)
   meditating.

The Old Lizard (El Lagarto Viejo)
Federico García Lorca 1898–1936

Table of Contents

 Preface

So much has gone on in my life since this book first saw print in 1997. It was my first book to be published and will always hold a special place in my heart. Now I'm a well-seasoned author of both fiction and nonfiction, firmly established in my career and much more confident as a writer. Since 1997, my life has been a roller coaster. At the time this book was first published, my husband and I were struggling financially; now we are more secure. During the past few years, my mother died from cancer, my stepfather is currently on his deathbed from cancer, my husband has been tentatively diagnosed with a rare disease (treatable but not curable), and the world feels like it's gone topsy-turvy. On the other hand, I'm much happier with all my publishers, I've sold a mystery series and am really enjoying writing novels, I've started my way on the long road back to health from an accident back in 1994, and this year I celebrate ten wonderful years of marriage to Samwise.

During the past six years since the first publication of this book, my view of religion has shifted dramatically. September 11 had a lot to do with this shift, and with my perception of religion in general. I must admit, I've become much more cynical, much more proactive about human rights versus religious rights. However, despite these changes, my spirituality has only intensified on an internalized level. I'm not talking about rituals, or about how I practice magic, or even about the fact that I no longer spell magic with a *k*.

No, what I'm saying is that I seldom refer to my spirituality as a religion anymore—it's simply settled into an integral part of my life path, a personal quest for understanding. Yes, I'm still a Witch, and my practice is much more shamanistic than it used to be. While I will always remain true to the core foundation on which my spirituality is based, and while my service to Mielikki and Tapio has become much more definitive and I no longer work within other traditions, my path in life remains an ever-changing, always-evolving spiritual quest, and that's how I want it to be.

So here we go with the new edition of this book. You may notice a few minor changes if you've read the first edition of this book; my writing is much tighter now, and I welcome this chance to clear up a few nagging mistakes that I noticed when *Trancing the Witch's Wheel* first came out.

If you wish to contact me, you may do so through my website, Galenorn En/Visions, at www.galenorn.com. I have a contact page there that explains how to email me. Or you may write to me in care of the publisher.

My journey into magic and meditation began several years before I ever cast my first spell, chanted my first chant, or pledged myself into the service of the Gods. I began college when I was fifteen years old, a restless and search-ing time for anyone. For me, the jump from junior high to college signified freedom from an oppressive educational system that had held back both my intellectual and social growth. Liberated from the repressive confines of high school, I was able to stretch my mind among people who actually wanted to be in school, who were as eager to learn as I. I no longer felt like an outcast; I had friends and I had knowledge. I truly felt that I had been let out of a cage, and it was in this atmosphere that I signed up for a Philosophy of Religion class.

I was undergoing a religious crisis at that point. I could no longer accept the religion I had grown up with, yet was too afraid to admit it, even to myself. I took the class with the hope of discovering some sort of resolution. A minister, I've forgotten to which denomination he belonged, taught the class. At first that made me nervous. I was trying to break out of the hierarchical religious structure, not to embrace it. However, he taught me the most important lesson I was to learn that year, or any other, when he told the class, "Question your beliefs, and if they don't hold up, get rid of them. Find out what works for you."

His words were the permission I needed. Like all words, they were magical, congealing thoughts into reality. With his advice as my guidepost, I began a four-year search. I looked into Buddhism and agnosticism, and eventually stumbled onto the New Age movement. From each set of beliefs, I gained more clarity about myself, but nothing fit just right. I knew I believed in something; I just didn't know what.

Then, in a soccer field at Evergreen State College on a cold February night (February 29, 1980—leap year day, no less), I met the Goddess under the ancient moon and have considered myself a Witch ever since. I worked alone for many years, culling what I could from the few books I could find. Most of my knowledge came through experimentation. Later, I began to meet and work with other Pagans and Witches, and eventually I began to teach what I had learned over the years. In doing so, I noticed that throughout all my studies, there was one common thread that provided a link between most belief systems. That link is the practice of meditation or trance work.

Thanks to all the time and practice I've invested in meditation and visualization, my magic works far more often than not. The practice of meditation has touched other areas of my life, as well. I'm disciplined with both my writing and with life in general. I can keep my attention focused on the more mundane tasks of life until they are done. Since I'm also a professional tarot reader, I must be able to slip into a mild trance at will when reading for a client. It's only through the continual practice of meditation that I'm able to do this. The use of meditation, especially guided meditations such as the ones contained in this book, has benefited my life considerably, and I know it can help you too.

—the Painted Panther
YASMINE GALENORN

How to Use This Book

In this book I present a series of guided meditations. A guided meditation, unlike many Eastern forms of meditation, leads you on a journey intended to stimulate your imagination and creativity. Instead of clearing or emptying your mind, your goal is to follow the journey that your guide presents to come to some clarity about yourself and your life.

This is achieved while you are in trance or in an altered state of consciousness. The meditation speaks directly to your Higher Self, to your subconscious mind. Within this inner self we discover the answers to many of our questions, as well as hidden talents and goals we may not realize we possess.

Unlike meditations that ask you to free your mind from all thought, guided meditation encourages you to use your mind, to stretch past limitations that keep you from realizing your full potential.

I have written these meditations for use in either a group or solitary setting. You can use them as inspiration, reading and pondering them as you might read poetry; you can tape-record them and play them back while you follow along. In a group setting, you can designate one person to be the guide. Since the meditations rely on self-hypnosis, you don't need anyone to help you.

Each meditation contains a section called "Guidelines for Use," which suggests altar dressings, incenses, flowers, and oils to enhance your experience. Following each meditation, the "Suggested Exercises" will help you make the most out of what you've learned through the meditation. I encourage you to experiment with them.

Before using it in practice, read the entire meditation thoroughly to familiarize yourself with it, especially if you are going to tape-record it or if you are the designated guide for a group.

If you use these meditations in a group setting, try to schedule time after the meditation for everyone to share their insights and discoveries. While no one should feel pressured, the mutual sharing of experience often leads to more understanding about the element, Sabbat, deity, or dimension being explored. If you are working within a group situation, I recommend that a different person lead each meditation so everyone gets a chance to go on a journey. An alternative is to tape-record each meditation, and then everyone in the group can listen to it together.

Notes for Readers and Guides

- If you are guiding a meditation, be aware that certain thoughts can trigger extreme emotional responses. You should watch the group carefully as you lead the meditation. If someone appears distressed, ask them quietly whether they need assistance. Usually they will be able to work through the problem without your help, but it pays to be observant.

- If you are tape-recording these meditations or guiding a group, at the end of each paragraph pause for a slow, silent count of five seconds, then continue. Where I have indicated a long pause in the text, pause for approximately thirty seconds. This should give those meditating plenty of time to contemplate the thoughts presented.

A Note of Caution

As I have said, these meditations are essentially self-hypnosis and as such, it would be dangerous to drive right after you have finished. *Take pains to include the last paragraph of each meditation, which should bring you out of the trance.* As an added suggestion, I recommend that, after practicing each meditation, you eat something light, preferably high in protein, to ground yourself in the mundane world once more.

About the Meditations in This Book

This book is divided into four sections. Part 1 includes a brief introduction to meditation in general, as well as Cleansing and Protecting and Grounding and Centering meditations.

Part 2 includes meditations on the elements, an in-depth journey through the four elements: Earth, Air, Fire, and Water. By exploring these, we can come to a better understanding of their place in our lives, our hearts, and our magic.

Part 3 includes meditations on the Sabbats, a journey through the Pagan Wheel of the Year, starting with Samhain and following the year around to Mabon. I have included a brief discussion of each Sabbat along with the meditation and exercises.

Part 4 explores deities and dimensions and includes various meditations I have written over the years for different rituals.

I have included correspondence tables (appendix 1), to which you can refer if you wish to explore a particular focus or theme in greater depth. For example, the Litha Meditation incorporates exploration of the Faerie Kingdom as well as the Summer Solstice. Appendix 2 is a supplies and resources guide.

A chakra chart and a glossary provide further clarification of terminology used throughout these meditations.

In closing, I can only repeat that meditation has had such an impact on my life that, with this book, I hope to pass on some of those transformations and joys to you.

May you have blessed journeys!

PART 1

The Basics
of Meditation

 Introduction to Meditation

Meditation is the art of contemplation. Simply put, to meditate is to focus on a particular thought or subject in order to achieve a predetermined goal. Just about every religion, and many secular orders, practice some form of meditation. Christianity, Islam, and Judaism have prayers. Zen and Ch'an Buddhists have *dhyana* (Sanskrit for "concentrated meditation") yoga practices. Islam has *dhikr*. Today, the terms *mantra* and *mandala* have become familiar. Transcendental Meditation, which was popularized during the 1970s, blends Eastern mysticism with Western practicality.

Some people use meditation as a form of prayer to elevate their consciousness and become closer to the God-form(s) they recognize; others use meditation to reduce stress and to let go of the fast-paced world surrounding them. Still others use it to explore their inner selves so they might live less-conflicted lives.

All of the above forms and reasons have their place, but many of the more religious-based practices take years of rigorous study and devotion to learn. In this book you will explore a form of meditation that just about anyone can practice, including children.

Your ultimate goal in learning to use guided meditations should be to hone your powers of visualization and concentration. Magic is a demanding practice, but the rewards can be substantial and, if done with proper intent, gratifying. Guided meditation makes magical practice easier. It helps you learn to focus your mind and thereby focus your will. Focused will, or energy, provides results.

Some other spiritual benefits from the regular use of guided meditation include heightened intuition, psychic dreams, better results from the spells you cast, and an enhanced sense of what I call *faerie sight* (the ability to see into other realms, i.e., the faerie realm or the mystical side of nature).

By heightening awareness through guided meditation, you will also find an increased ability to concentrate while studying, reading, and completing mundane tasks. You can create short- and long-term goals and use guided meditation to help you achieve them.

Many forms of meditation stress that emptying the mind of all extraneous thought is the way to peace and tranquillity. While that may be true, our goal in this book is to learn how to visualize and use concentrated focus to affect our lives and bring about changes in consciousness.

Shall we begin?

Exercises in Preparation for Meditation

Loosening the Body Exercise

Make sure your clothes are comfortable. Loosen any tight straps or binding fasteners.

Take three deep breaths.

Stand up and reach up toward the ceiling. (You can do this while sitting in a chair, if necessary. Just adapt the movements to what you can do.) Keeping your right foot flat on the ground to bear your weight, stretch toward the ceiling with your left side, arm raised and taut, hand splayed. Point your left leg in front of you and stretch your leg and foot so only the toes of your left foot touch the ground. Hold for a count of five. Slowly lower your foot to the ground and draw your leg back.

Now reach up with your right side, arm raised and taut, hand splayed. This time, allow your left foot to bear your weight. Extend your right leg and stretch as before, holding for a count of five. Slowly lower your foot to the floor and draw your leg back.

Next, gently drop your arms to your sides. Lean to your left, as if the floor was pulling your arm down. Hold for a count of five. Slowly come up again and repeat on the right side.

Now gently bend forward from the waist and let your arms dangle in front of you. Bend your knees—you should not feel any pain while doing this—and shake your body gently from side to side. Now raise up again.

Take three deep breaths.

Examine how your body feels now. When you are meditating, you must be able to relax so your focus can be entirely on the journey in front of you. The above exercise is a gentle way to let go of tension and prepare yourself for meditation. It is also helpful anytime you need to take a break from a stressful situation.

Listening to the Breath Exercise

Make sure you are wearing comfortable clothing and that you have privacy for at least ten minutes. Take a moment to do the *Loosening the Body Exercise* and then sit in a comfortable position. Take three deep breaths.

As you let out the third breath, close your eyes. Now sit still, breathing normally, but listen to your breath as you take it in, and then as you let it out. Feel your lungs expand as you inhale and feel them contract as you exhale. Breathe through your mouth. Does it feel different from when you breathe through your nose? Each time your mind starts to wander, stop, gently bring your focus back to your breathing, and start again. Practice this for five minutes, then take another three deep breaths and open your eyes.

It can help to set a timer so you know when the five minutes are over. You will probably find that the time drags at first. Five minutes can be a long time when you aren't used to focusing on one subject. Practice the *Listening to the Breath Exercise* once or twice a day for a week and discover what differences you notice.

Taste Test Exercise

On a tray, arrange a slice of lemon, a piece of chocolate, a whole lemon, and a wrapped chocolate bar.

Sit in a comfortable position with a large glass of water nearby. Take three deep breaths. Now pick up the lemon. Look at it closely. Feel its weight and texture. Set the lemon down and pick up the slice of lemon. Close your eyes and bite into the slice. Feel the juice explode in your mouth. Notice how your face responds to the taste—what muscles tense up? What is your expression? Explore the taste of the fruit. Is it hard to chew or does it slide easily down your throat? When you are finished, take a drink of the water to clear the taste from your mouth.

Now pick up the chocolate bar. Examine the wrapper. Notice the wording on it, the color of the paper. Is it wrapped in gold or silver foil? Is the bar heavy or is it light? Now pick up the piece of chocolate and slip it onto your tongue. Let it melt a little; feel the pressure as you carefully bite into it. What does the taste do for you? What is it like? Is the chocolate plain, or does it have something in it?

When you are finished, set the tray aside. Now close your eyes and visualize the lemon. Cup your hand and try to re-create the feeling of holding it. How heavy was it? Can you recall the texture? How bright was the skin? Now remember the slice of lemon. Mentally bite down on it. Does your expression respond to the sour taste? Try to re-create the sensation of eating the lemon slice.

Next, remember the chocolate bar. Can you recall what the wrapping said? Can you see the candy bar in your mind? What color is the foil? Is it sealed or folded around the chocolate? Unwrap it in your mind. Break off a bite of the chocolate and place it on your tongue. How fast does it melt? What does it taste like?

When you are done, take three deep breaths and open your eyes.

The purpose of this exercise was to learn to re-create senses in your mind, to stimulate your imagination. To be most effective, the journeys in guided meditations must encompass as many senses as possible. Therefore, the more you can re-create in your mind what you experience in reality, the deeper your trance will be and the more effective your meditation will become.

Favorite Song Exercise

We've all had the experience of suddenly realizing that an advertising jingle or a song we heard on the radio is still running through our minds. The purpose of this exercise is to re-create that experience.

Obtain a good, clear recording of your favorite song. For our purposes here, it should be catchy and have both lyrics and music.

Make yourself comfortable. Take three deep breaths and turn on the song. Close your eyes and listen to it all the way through. Rewind the tape. Stand up while playing the song a second time. While keeping your eyes closed, move gently in response to the rhythm.

When you finish listening to the song a second time, sit down and close your eyes. Visualize yourself pressing the button to rewind the tape, and then pressing another to play it. Hear the song. Don't try to force yourself to remember every word, just let the music pour out of your mind. If you feel like moving to the music in your head, go ahead. If your mind starts to wander, mentally pause the tape, bring your attention back, then allow the song to continue. When you are finished playing the song back to yourself, take three deep breaths and open your eyes.

Being able to listen to your inner self while undergoing a guided meditation is very important. Words have power; words are magical. If we cannot hear ourselves at a subconscious level, then we have lost our most important guide. Your subconscious mind contains the answers to many of your philosophical, as well as mundane, questions. It encompasses the self-knowledge that allows us to be autonomous creatures. Spirit guides and gurus are fine, but our best and first mentor should be our own self. No one should make decisions for you. We must be able to access our inner voices to be holistic, centered beings.

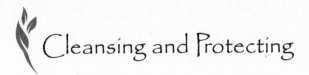 Cleansing and Protecting

In this chapter, I offer a simple but effective Cleansing and Protecting meditation. The section called "Guidelines for Use" suggests various crystals, flowers, and other accoutrements that you might want to have nearby during your meditation. You may choose to set up a small altar for use during your meditation. Feel free to use all of my suggestions or none, or to create your own traditions. I recommend making your meditation a special time, and the use of flowers, scents, and crystals can accentuate this.

Guidelines for Use

This meditation is appropriate anytime we feel the need to clear our thoughts, or when we are feeling vulnerable and want to feel stronger. I recommend taking a bath in warm water with lavender bath salts or bubble bath before performing this meditation.

You might also wish to smudge yourself before you begin the meditation. Smudging is an ancient form of purification that aids in altering consciousness. I highly recommend it before meditating, and I recommend the use of white sage or cedar, though other incenses will work. Just use something appropriate to the individual meditation.

To smudge yourself, light the incense or smudge stick (a bundle of sacred herbs) and wave the smoke over your body, inhaling deeply. As you exhale, let go of tension and stress. To smudge someone else, have them stand while you wave the smoke around their body. You can use your hand or a large feather to guide the smoke. Try to let the smoke touch all chakra points (see the chakra chart in the appendix). Then trade places. Just be careful not to touch the person with the burning herb or catch their hair on fire.

If you are allergic to smoke, you can produce a similar effect by aspirging, or spraying lightly with water in which sacred herbs have been sitting. To aspirge, steep a cedar branch or lavender flowers in warm water for ten minutes, then strain. Use the cedar branch to gently flick droplets of the water over yourself. The drops of water carry the purifying essence of the herbs. Be cautious not to flick the water onto paintings or books or other objects that might not take too well to water stains. You can use both aspirging and smudging in the same meditation, if you like.

FLOWERS: *lavender sprig, white carnation, white rose*
INCENSES: *lavender, cedar, sage, pine*
OILS: *lavender, rosemary, rose geranium*
CRYSTALS: *amethyst, blue agate, sapphire, aquamarine*
CANDLES: *blue, white, lavender*

Cleansing and Protecting Meditation

Relax. Sit back and make sure you are in a comfortable position.

Now close your eyes and take three deep breaths.

You are standing on a path, looking toward a large forest. The sun is up; it is midmorning, and it's the sort of day that makes you want to find a warm meadow in which you can lie and look at the clouds. The color of the sky is rich with blue, and tiny white streaks of clouds lazily drift by. They are so far up, you can barely see them.

A sparrow darts by, then another. You watch them for a minute, then turn your attention to the path in front of you.

A long path, it's narrow and worn, as if many feet have walked here before. It leads to the forest, and you feel a pull urging you forward. There is something in the forest that sings out your name. Though you want nothing more than to relax, you decide to follow the call and see where it leads you.

Step onto the path and begin walking toward the forest.

Long Pause

The grass to either side of the path is dry; the summer sun has dried it until it's like straw, withered yellow and harsh on the skin. Looking at it makes you feel parched, and you wonder if the rains will come again to replenish the earth.

Follow the path as it leads you to the edge of the forest. There, the cool shade from the cedars and oaks standing sentinel promises a welcome relief from the intense heat that is rising as noon approaches. As you step onto the path that leads through the forest, the shelter of the branches provides instant comfort.

Look around to get your bearings. You notice small animals peering out of the undergrowth. Here a rabbit watches you, nose twitching and ready to bolt. There, under a huckleberry, a robin searches for a worm. A squirrel is climbing a nearby cedar and stops for a moment to look you over, then continues on its way. Look around and see what else you can find in the undergrowth.

Long Pause

Now continue along the path. As you go deeper into the woods, a sense of calmness, of peace, begins to descend around your shoulders like a cloak, muffling whatever tensions you have brought with you. The silence is comforting, a hush that stills the chatter in your mind. Listen quietly as you walk among the cedars.

These trees must have been growing for hundreds of years, you think. They are huge, old with gnarled faces in their bark, and they watch you gently as you pass by. Some of the faces smile; others just watch silently, noting your passage. These are sentinels, guardians of the forest, and they will not allow anything or anyone to disrupt their realm. You are safe as you walk among them.

Long Pause

Now the forest thickens as the path narrows even further, and you wonder if it is ever going to end. You are considering turning back when you see, up ahead, the end of the path, with an opening into a meadow.

Ivy twines down the oaks that guard the portal. You see the vines twist around the trunks; they are alive. They move and sway in the breeze, but as you approach they pull back so you may enter.

Step through the opening and find yourself in a large, bowl-shaped lea. It is a meadow of immense proportions. It might have been, in a time long past, a giant crater on a volcano, or an ancient lake long dried up and vanished. But now it is filled with grass the color of peridot, sparkling green and lush with dew that has not yet dried. Wildflowers dot the meadow, burgundy and fuchsia, yellow, and vivid orange. You can smell their scents on the light breeze around you.

Long Pause

In the center of the meadow you see a small pond. The water sparkles as sunlight finds its way through the opening in the wooded glen, reflecting like diamonds and palest sapphires. Water lilies float on the surface, and frogs croak from the shore.

It's very warm now that you are no longer shaded by the trees, and though the forest continues on the other side, you feel that this pond is what called you. Approach the water and look at it for a moment.

The pond is cool; it radiates peace, and you feel that if you could only touch it, slide into the shimmering liquid, it would wash away all the tension, care, and worry that permeates your everyday existence.

Long Pause

Slowly remove your clothes and drape them over a nearby bush. Don't be afraid or ashamed; there's no one here to see you. As you undress, a big fuzzy bumblebee flies by on a drunken flight from flower to flower, first landing on some Indian paintbrush, then flying to a patch of cornflowers, and finally making its way to a daisy.

Step to the edge of the water. Sit down on the grass and dangle your feet in the pool. The water has been warmed by the sun and, though it is refreshing, it doesn't chill you. The pond is shallow. You can slide in and sit with your back against the bank without immersing your head.

Slide into the water and make yourself comfortable. Lean back and close your eyes.

Long Pause

Something tickles your feet and as you sit up to look, you notice tiny fish darting in and out around your toes. They appear to be kissing you, and then you realize that they are like the fish that follow the dolphins and whales; they are cleaning your body. As they gently remove dirt and grime off of your legs and arms, they also suck the tension from your muscles. Lean forward so they can reach your back and shoulders.

When they're finished and have left, you notice that a lily pad is floating near you. Something shiny is on the flower. It's dusted with a sparkling powder. Take a little of the powder in your hand and wet it. It lathers up, foaming with bubbles. As you begin to wash your body with the foam, it tingles against your skin, energizing and revitalizing wherever it touches.

Wash your body and face with the lather and then dip under the pond to rinse it off your skin.

Long Pause

After you wipe the water out of your eyes, you hear a croaking nearby and turn to see a frog sitting on the shore near your clothes. Next to the frog is a crystal goblet, and in the goblet is a golden liquid that shines like the sun.

"Welcome to my pond," the frog says. "All who need healing and cleansing may come and take refuge in my crystal waters."

Step out of the pond and let the sun's warm light begin to dry your body. The frog watches carefully as you kneel down so you can talk to it more easily.

"I am the guardian of the pond," the frog says. "You have cleansed yourself in my waters, now would you drink from my goblet?"

You ask the frog what the liquid is, and the frog motions for you to pick up the chalice.

"The golden liqueur within this goblet is the wine of inner strength and self-confidence; it is the nectar of all who would live their truths. Think about yourself for a moment, about the ways in which you would like to be a stronger person, about the truth of your heart and the ways in which you would like to walk your life path. Then hold those images firmly in mind; drink from the chalice, and the golden nectar will fill your veins and help you manifest your desires."

Take a moment to think about what the frog said, then when you are ready, drink the wine.

Extended Long Pause—about two minutes

As you drink, the wine races down your throat like liquid sunshine. It spills into your bloodstream and fills you with inner strength, with vitality and healing rays of warmth.

You look at the world around you, and now you seem more solid, more substantial, cleansed and capable of handling any situation that may arise in your life.

Long Pause

The frog says, "Anytime you need to feel purified and protected, you may return to my pool and bathe in the cleansing waters. I will be here to greet you, and you may rest in the silence that allows you to listen to your soul. Go now, back to your world, and remember, I am always here if you need me."

Say good-bye to the frog as it hops away. Your clothes are lying in a neat pile, and as you put them on, you find that they, too, have been cleaned. The faint hint of cedar lingers in the cloth, and as you dress, it feels as though you are wearing a shield of protection.

When you have dressed, take another look at the pond, then turn back to the path. The sun is waning; it's late afternoon, and as you glide through the trees, you still feel small animals watching, waiting until you are gone to come out and hunt or drink.

Long Pause

You traverse the path quickly, feeling much lighter on your feet than you did when you first entered the forest. Soon, you are standing on the edge of the wood, and you see, in the distance, the place from which you first journeyed.

Listen to my voice. As I count from twenty backward to one, you will retrace your steps, becoming more alert and aware with each passing number. Twenty . . . nineteen . . . the sun is slowly descending in the sky . . . eighteen . . . seventeen . . . sixteen . . . you are starting to become aware of the world around you . . . fifteen . . . fourteen . . . thirteen . . . you are nearing the place where you began this journey . . . twelve . . . eleven . . . ten . . . you are becoming alert and aware . . . nine . . . eight . . . as you wake to full consciousness you will feel refreshed and totally alert . . . seven . . . six . . . your eyes are beginning to open . . . five . . . four . . . three . . . take one deep breath . . . two . . . take another deep breath and let it out slowly . . . one . . . you are back to the beginning . . . take a third deep breath, let it out, and when you are ready, you may open your eyes.

Suggested Exercises for Cleansing and Protecting Meditation

1. Take a few moments to think about the inner strengths you desire. What are some ways that you can manifest them?

2. If you feel a need for more protection or safety in your life, are there practical steps that you can take to achieve this?

3. Sometimes a meditation like this can leave us feeling a little sad or melancholy. This is often because we feel safe and protected while in the meditation, but when we come out we are back in a world of violence and anger. If this happened to you, is there some way you can make your personal environment feel more cozy, more inviting and safe? Often, a change in color schemes can help, rearranging the furniture, getting new locks for the doors, making herbal charms to drive away the negativity; there are many things you can do. Use your creativity and imagination.

4. Ask each person in the group to share what their interpretation of the forest was like. It is interesting to note the variations people will create with their minds. Sometimes something will appear in a meditation that has nothing to do with the suggestions presented, but it should not be dismissed. The person meditating needs to examine that image to determine what it means to them and why it appeared.

Grounding and Centering

It is important with any type of magical or metaphysical work to retain some control over oneself and to keep an anchor in the world around you. I define this as grounding and centering.

Grounding connects your energy with the world around you so you can be an effective conduit for any energy you might raise during meditation or ritual. It keeps you from getting scattered and flighty.

Centering balances your energy, your emotions, your body, and your mind in preparation for metaphysical work.

If you do not ground and center yourself, your meditations will not be as effective as they could otherwise be.

Guidelines for Use

This meditation is appropriate anytime you feel out of balance, or when you are preparing for a major magical working. It is a good meditation to use on a regular basis, perhaps at the beginning of the week or on every full and new moon.

I recommend that you use the *Loosening the Body Exercise* first, then the *Listening to the Breath Exercise*, before you use the *Grounding and Centering Meditation*. You might also want to smudge yourself with sage or sweet grass.

PLANTS: *sage, sweet grass, cedar, patchouli, oakmoss*
INCENSES: *sage, sweet grass, cedar*
OILS: *earth, oakmoss, cypress, cedar*
CRYSTALS: *hematite, tiger's-eye, aventurine, calcite*
CANDLES: *yellow, white, brown*

Grounding and Centering Meditation

Relax and make yourself comfortable.

Close your eyes and take three deep breaths.

It is twilight, and you are standing on the top of a tall mesa. The mountain rises up hundreds of feet above the ocean. Behind you is a wide swath of grass, still warm from the day, and a large oak tree stands near, dripping with leaves. In the far distance, you see the silhouette of a forest, indistinct and a very long way away.

There is a light breeze blowing. It feels good against your skin.

As you watch, the first stars begin to shimmer into view. The night is clear, and you notice the last birds fly past, eagerly winging home for the night.

Long Pause

You have come to this place to regain your balance with the world around you, to find your central core, from which you wisely guide your actions and words. You have come here to draw from the power of the Earth and from the power of the stars.

Walk over to the oak and examine it. See all its gnarled branches, the bulging roots that push their way out of the ground. Notice the long dripping moss that hangs to the ground like an ancient lace veil.

Run your fingers over the bark; examine the cracks and crevices that bespeak the oak's age. Let your hand sweep over cobwebs and dirt; let your fingers rest on soft pads of thick moss and lichen.

Long Pause

Press your nose to the oak and inhale; smell the ancient wood, the life that still vibrates within its limbs and branches. Breathe deeply and pull its essence into your lungs.

Can you sense its strength? Its vitality?

Long Pause

Whisper your name to the oak.

Now ask the oak what it is called and whether it has a message for you. Listen well for its answer.

Long Pause

A noise from an upper branch startles you. An owl is watching you with its great golden eyes. It drops out of the tree and soundlessly glides past. As it does, one feather falls from its wing. The feather drifts down on the breeze to land at your feet. Pick it up and examine it. Look carefully at the pattern.

Long Pause

Now move a few steps away from the oak. Take off your shoes, if you are wearing any, and plant your feet firmly on the warm soil.

From your feet, roots spring and grow, like the roots of the oak. They burrow deep into the soil, pressing down through dirt and pebbles, burrowing deeper and deeper.

Long Pause

Inhale slowly.

Exhale.

As you breathe out, the roots from your feet grow longer, extending like tendrils of a vine, exploring the soil, pressing deeper, deeper through the ground.

Down they go, through rock and soil, reaching farther, stretching, rooting you solidly as they seek and search.

Farther and farther, see them grow, burrowing through cavern and crystal, through rock and stone, down through land that in ages past once stood exposed to the air.

Long Pause

These roots, they grow down farther and farther, through the crust of the Earth, down through its mantle.

Farther and farther they stretch, until they break through and touch the core of the world, the molten, glowing heart of the Earth.

When they dip into that glowing magma, that sun-bright liquid, they begin to draw energy from the lava, from the heart of the world, and it climbs up, through the soil, through rock and mantle, through cavern and crystal.

Long Pause

Energy rises through pebble and dirt, surging up through your roots, seeking, rushing until it pours into your feet like a golden dream.

Feel the rush of warmth in your feet, rising through your ankles and calves, rooting you solidly into the strength that is the Earth.

Now it rises into your thighs, then into your groin, spreading through your abdomen, warm and fluid, strong and vibrant.

Long Pause

The energy surges again, flooding your torso, pouring down your arms, into your wrists and hands. Your arms rise with the energy, lifting over your head to stretch toward the heavens. The glowing warmth fills your head and pushes up through your crown chakra. You are glowing, golden and vibrant with the strength of the Earth.

Long Pause

Now look up, toward the stars.

One, brighter than the rest and glowing pale, crystal blue, shimmers and a thin slice of light, a sliver of energy, shoots out from the star and races toward Earth.

Down it comes, as you watch, down through the atmosphere, clear and pure and icy and, like a lightning bolt, it touches the tips of your fingers. The energy is cold. It is the ancient celestial music that hums between the stars; it is the pure, clear note of a crystal; it is the ice that does not melt, the energy of keen thought, of perfect intent.

It traces a path down through your fingertips, down through your wrists into your hands. It enters your crown chakra and floods your mind with clarity and clear purpose.

Long Pause

Like a cloud, the energy billows through your heart and torso, clearing away old hurts and cobwebs chaining you to the past.

Long Pause

The clear, blue force slices through your legs, through your ankles and feet, and you feel free, aware, and in control.

The glowing energy from the Earth meets the celestial energy from the stars, and they mix and intertwine, each finding the area of your body and soul that needs it most. They are not alien to one another, but partners, and together they balance your energy.

Extended Long Pause—about two minutes

Now the celestial energy begins to pull out, back toward the stars. It rises up and, like an arrow, is gone.

Long Pause

The glowing magma of the Earth boils back down, through your roots, through soil and pebble and rock and crystal, through cavern and mantle to the core from which it sprang.

Long Pause

Take three deep breaths. Feel the balance that both energies left within you. Feel the strength of your roots. They do not weigh you down, but give you security and a foundation on which to base your life.

Long Pause

Walk away from the oak, back to the edge of the mesa. Look into the darkening sky and know that, even as the Earth is your home, the foundation from which your body sprang, the stars are a source of clear thought and mental awakening. You can tap both Earth and Sky for balance.

Long Pause

Now, as I count from twenty to one, you will become awake and alert, and the feeling of balance will stay with you as you go about your daily life. Twenty . . . nineteen . . . eighteen . . . seventeen . . . you are becoming more alert . . . sixteen . . . fifteen . . . fourteen . . . thirteen . . . the sounds around you are becoming clearer . . . twelve . . . eleven . . . ten . . . nine . . . you are becoming aware of the world around you . . . eight . . . seven . . . six . . . five . . . four . . . you will awake clear and refreshed . . . three . . . two . . . one . . . take three deep breaths, and when you are ready, you may open your eyes.

Suggested Exercises for
Grounding and Centering Meditation

1. When you are feeling out of balance, it is often due to not living your truth. Examine your everyday life. Are you living in accordance with what you believe? Are there specific routines or practices you can change to give you a better sense of balance?

2. If your job is excessively physical or excessively mental, chances are you will be out of balance. You can actively prevent this by balancing your work with your play. Look at your life. Do you need more exercise? Do you need more time reading and thinking? You can make a difference if you choose to.

3. When you are in a crisis, you must be grounded to avoid exacerbating the situation. Think of times when you could have handled a situation better if you were grounded. Now think of times when you did handle a situation well because you remained in control of yourself. Examine ways that you might be able to avoid losing control in the future.

PART 2

Meditations on
the Elements

# Earth

To delve into Witchcraft, Wicca, Paganism, or any earth-centric spirituality, you must first understand the elements with which you will be working. In the majority of these traditions, working with the four elements (earth, air, fire, and water) remains a constant factor. One way to understand these elements is through the use of guided meditations. We begin with Earth, the northern watchtower. I always cast my magical circles from the north (as opposed to the traditional east) because I like to ground them in the earth first. The north, or Earth, is traditionally the direction associated with manifestation, materialization, stability, prosperity, security, the physical body, and strength. In northern European Paganism, it is often associated with the winter months and with midnight.

The element of Earth reminds us of our mortality, of our lives as physical beings. We are here on this planet to experience life in a body, to experience life as a finite being at this time. We must remember, in all the search for transcendence going on right now, that if we ignore the lessons to be learned through mortal life we will have to do it all over again the next time around. Life is to be experienced and enjoyed.

Guidelines for Use

This meditation is appropriate whenever you want to connect with the physical world around you.

I recommend that you use the *Loosening the Body Exercise* before performing the Earth Meditation. I also recommend holding a piece of fur, a branch off a tree, a crystal, or a piece of bone to connect you with Earth energy, since these are commonly associated with that element.

PLANTS: *sweet grass, red rose, chrysanthemum*
INCENSES: *pine, rose, patchouli, sandalwood*
OILS: *rose, patchouli, earth, sandalwood, musk*
CRYSTALS: *hematite, tiger's-eye, petrified wood, agate*
CANDLES: *brown, green*

Earth Meditation

Relax and make yourself comfortable.

Close your eyes and take three deep breaths.

You are standing on the edge of a forest, at the beginning of a dirt path. The night sky stretches overhead with stars sprinkling across the vast expanse. Now take another deep breath and step onto the path.

The forest grows thick around you as you journey, dark silhouettes of cedar, alder, and fir reaching toward the sky. As you look up at their towering stature, you notice a faint green aura surrounding them. Go over to one huge, ancient cedar and place your hands on the trunk. Press your ear against the bark and listen. Hear the sap rising; this is the blood of the earth. Listen to the murmur as the tree creaks in the wind. Hundreds of years old, and yet it is young in the eons of the Earth.

Long Pause

Now slide your hands down the trunk until you are touching the ground. Thick layers of leaf mulch and dried needles cover the base of the tree. Pick up a handful and bring it to your nose. Inhale a deep breath of the sour, tangy scent of the earth.

You decide to go back to the path and continue on. Noises dart in and out of the forest as you pass. Once, a deer stares at you from a patch of bracken. Another time, you startle a bird and see the faint blur of wings as it soars into the sky.

The path ascends as the forest falls away. You are walking up a dry, barren slope now, with patches of grass, pale and silver in the night, scattered at your feet. Your legs begin to ache and your breath comes hard; the incline is very steep. But now you can see your destination—a small, dark cave opening at the top of the hill.

Long Pause

You must use both your hands and feet to push yourself up the last stretch. Grab hold of rocks jutting out from the cliff and, in one last pull, scramble up to the ledge by the cave opening.

Rest for a minute in front of the dark opening that leads into the mountain. The ledge is firm, wide enough to sit on. As you sprawl on the rocky surface, think about why you have come on this journey. You've heard the legends of the King of Earth who lives deep within the sacred mountain, and you've heard tales of his crystalline cave that sparkles with energy. You have come to learn about the powers of the soil and the strength that lies among the bones of the world.

Long Pause

Rested, stand and take three slow, deep breaths, then enter the cavern.

Pause to let your eyes adjust. As the darkness gives way to dim shadows, you begin to notice a faint sparkle of light on the walls of the shaft. It lights your path, just enough for you to see. Run your fingers across the stone and bring them away. You can see a faint shimmer of light twinkling on your skin. This is faerie fire, the fire with no heat that burns green and golden in the night.

A cough startles you and you turn around. In front of you stands a small person, shorter than your knee. He is sturdy and dressed in browns and greens, and a long beard curls from his chin. He wears a cap of moss and carries a gnarled staff in his hand.

He looks at you, eyes the dark brown of the soil, and says, "I am your guide to the realms of the Earth. I will take you to meet the King of Earth, who lives at the center of the world. Do you need anything before we go? A staff? An animal companion? If so, ask for it, and it will appear."

Take a moment to decide whether there is anything you need for this journey.

Long Pause

"Now," he says, "we are ready to begin. Follow me." He leads you down a narrow, sloping passage in the back of the cavern. It is close, with loose rocks underfoot, and you must be cautious as you follow the gnome, for it would be easy to slip here.

You journey in silence for what seems like hours, your guide always a few feet ahead of you. As you follow him, you feel yourself slipping further and further into trance, going deep within yourself as you go deep within the Earth. Each step takes you farther into the element that you have come to explore.

Long Pause

After a time, the gnome stops. He points to the cavern wall. You look and see, in the compressed earth and stone, pottery shards and rotten wood.

"People lived here once," he says. "They made things from the earth, of clay and wood, and when they died, they left these behind. But someday these shards will dissolve back into their original elements." Reach up and touch one of the pieces of pottery; see what it has to tell you about where it came from.

Long Pause

He motions to you. "Come, we have a long way to go." As you pass through the layers of time, you see pictures drawn in stone on the cavern walls. These layers of earth were once exposed to light but now reside deep in the mountainside. You journey for a while longer and then he stops once more, pointing to a human skeleton that lies frozen in soil.

"The flesh is long gone, back to the earth; the bones take longer. They are roots in this world. Look at the bones, then look at your own hands and know that inside of your body, your own skeleton stands strong, roots holding you up and together. Know that each person has their time and then returns to the earth. You may return to life many times, but each time, your body returns to the soil."

Long Pause

Once again, the gnome motions for you to follow him. You pass through a forest of stalagmites and stalactites, weaving around and through the pointed calcium deposits. And then into another passage and onward, still descending. You notice the walls now show a dinosaur skeleton and the fossilized leaves of a tree. "All part of the earth," the gnome says. "All parts of the whole."

When you think you can go no farther, when your legs are aching, he turns to you and says, "We're almost there. You see that opening ahead? It leads across the river of lava to the palace of the king. This is as far as I go. You must journey alone from here." And as suddenly as he appeared, the gnome is gone.

A sense of anticipation rushes over you. From where you stand, you hear the beating of drums, and the reverberations seem to echo through the very stone beneath your feet. Take three deep breaths and pass through the opening.

Long Pause

You are standing in a great cavern, so vast you can't begin to see the other side. Before you runs a river of lava. It boils and twists in its long journey, rushing past at a frightening momentum. There is a narrow stone archway with steps leading up to it, and this is the bridge over which you must pass. On the other side, you see a palace made of crystal. It sparkles in the light from the river of molten fire, and you can see from here glints of amethyst and emerald, of citrine and ruby and sapphire.

Climb the stairs to the arch. The stone bridge is narrow, with only a thin rail for a handhold, but it seems sturdy and weathered with time. As you cross the bridge, the lava hisses and crackles underneath.

Long Pause

On the other side, you find another staircase and descend. You are near the door of the palace, and it swings open as you approach. The drumming grows louder, and as you enter through the quartz arch, you realize the drumming is actually your own heartbeat matching rhythm with that of the Earth's.

Once inside, you find yourself in a room that seems to fill up the entire palace. In the center of the room resides a throne made of granite and quartz, and atop that throne sits a being. He is huge, with skin as knobby as bark, muscles carved out of gnarled wood, and a face as ageless as the Earth from which he draws his primal power. You are facing the King of Earth, the Lord of the North.

Long Pause

He motions you over to his side and says, "I am the King of Earth. I serve Great Mother Gaia. You have come to meet me; you have come to learn the mysteries of the soil."

He gives you a basket. "Look within," he says. In the basket you find a blade of grass, a slender oak branch, a peach, a bone, a crystal, a bowl of salt, a bowl of earth, a rose, and a piece of fur.

Long Pause

"Pick up the blade of grass," he says. "Examine it, feel the sharp edge, look at this, the hair of the Goddess; break it and smell it. Run it through your teeth." Now take the blade of grass and ask it to reveal its secrets to you."

Long Pause

"Next, take up the oak branch. Feel the strength that resides within this wood. Hold it, close your eyes, and see the tree from which it came. Know that oak is the root of the world; it is the strongest and most sacred tree. Ask to see its mysteries."

Long Pause

The King of Earth laughs. "Isn't it marvelous?" he says. "Isn't it all so wonderful? Now take up the peach and bite into the fruit, feel the sweetness of its being and know that this is provided to sustain you and the animals who feed upon the fruits of the Earth."

Long Pause

"Now look at the bone; it is the stone of your body and reminds the world that you were here. But it, too, passes as time goes by."

Long Pause

"And the crystal concentrates the powers of the Earth. Each stone contains a different essence."

Long Pause

"Now, take up the bowl of salt and know that this represents the element of Earth in your magic. Take a single grain and taste it on your tongue."

Long Pause

"And now," the King of Earth says, "take up the fur. All animals are an extension of the Earth, as are trees, as are rocks, as are your own bodies, all interconnected, all physical."

Long Pause

"When you pick up the bowl of earth, smell the rich, vibrant, fertile soil that grows all fruits and livestock to sustain your body. Understand that it provides the womb for the life that you know. Without this, without the dirt beneath your feet, you would not live. Without the soil, you would not exist."

Long Pause

Now look up into his swirling eyes, into eyes as green and vibrant as the brilliant feathers of a parakeet, look into that ancient and gnarled face that contains wisdom, compassion, and an ever-present core of iron and steel, and know that you are looking into a mirror, for all life is intertwined, and every tree, every flower that you look at, is a reflection of yourself.

Long Pause

"Lastly," he says, "take up the rose; look in its center, and see the mystery of Earth, of beauty caught in material form. Inhale, and learn what it is you came here to learn. This is my gift to you."

As you look into the rose, its fragrance wafts up, bringing with it strength and groundedness, and grace and beauty in movement. Take three deep breaths, drawing the essence of the rose into you, and listen for what it has to teach you.

Extended Long Pause—about two minutes

Now the King of Earth smiles at you and says, "It's time you left here. You must return to your body and the world above. There's a staircase behind my throne; it will lead you to the surface. Go now and remember what you have learned here." And he bids you farewell. If you have anything you'd like to say to him before you go, do so now.

Long Pause

Now step behind the throne, where you find a spiral staircase. It is carved first of crystal as you begin to ascend. The railing is strong, and even though you have a long way to climb, the stairs are wide and smooth and easy to traverse. Climb the stairs, see them circle around . . . now you are out of the palace, and the stairwell is going straight through the Earth itself. You climb . . . counting as you go, one count equaling ten stairs.

Twenty . . . the stairs are crystal and clear . . . nineteen . . . eighteen . . . the stairs are now granite and black . . . seventeen . . . sixteen . . . fifteen . . . fourteen . . . the stairs are now bone and you are beginning to become aware of other things around you . . . thirteen . . . twelve . . . you feel your body begin to wake up . . . eleven . . . the stairs are now tree roots . . . ten . . . nine . . . eight . . . you are beginning to feel alive and vibrant . . . seven . . . six . . . five . . . you see light coming from above . . . four . . . the stairs are made of oak and you are almost to the top . . . you are regaining your normal awareness . . . three . . . you see that you are coming up into an oak tree and two steps will lead you to the door . . . two . . . the steps are made of grass . . . one . . . the last step brings you to the door. Open the door, and you find you are back at the edge of the forest where you started. You are awake and alert. Take three deep breaths, and when you are ready, you may open your eyes.

Suggested Exercises for Earth Meditation

1. Spend some time each day for the following week focusing on the element of Earth. Pay attention to the trees and plants that surround you. Get out each day for a walk.
2. Gather together a piece of fur, a bone, a crystal, a small bowl full of soil, a branch, and a plant. After the meditation, let each person in the group hold each object for a brief time. Share impressions of the different energies after focusing on each object.

3. Spend time with your body during the following week. Exercise, bathe, and moisturize your skin. Get to know the feel of being in tune with your physical self.

4. Have safe sex with yourself or another person with whom you have a positive connection. Concentrate on the physicality of your being during this time.

Air

We began our journey through the elements by delving deep into the earth. Next, we will soar eastward, into the clouds, to explore the element of Air.

The element of Air is associated with intellect, insight, clarity of vision and goals, cleansing and purification, and new beginnings. It is often associated with dawn and the season of spring.

The element of Air reminds us that we are also thinking beings. We can make choices based on logic and reason. We invent and create; sometimes our inventions are wonderful, other times they become nightmares. The mind is like a computer, and we must exercise it to prevent stagnation. If we do not use healthy common sense, if we become gullible, then we are wasting a great gift.

Unfortunately, over the years I have met many wonderful people who have not learned how to question the events that happen in their lives. They have not learned to discern between what is a logical progression of events and what is truly miraculous.

We who practice any form of metaphysical work, be it magic or meditation, must be skeptical. We must not believe everything we read or hear. I shudder when I meet people who send hundreds of dollars to someone promising to cast a spell for them so they will win the lottery or gain the love they so desperately seek. They do not believe that they can effect changes in their own lives. Quite often, these people need professional counseling instead of a Witch. The mind recognizes destructive patterns in our lives if we have the proper tools with which to identify them. In many cases, the solution to a problem is easy once the actual difficulty has been identified.

If we are not willing to use common sense, then we have no business practicing magic or working with metaphysical forces. These powers are very real, and we must be intelligent enough to use them wisely.

Guidelines for Use

This meditation is appropriate whenever you want to connect with your intellect, whenever you want clarity on an issue, or when you are beginning a new project. I recommend using this meditation before you have to study for an important test.

I recommend that you use the *Loosening the Body Exercise* first, then the *Listening to the Breath Exercise*, before performing this meditation. I also recommend holding a feather while you meditate. If you can use an electric fan during the meditation, the circulating air seems to help.

PLANTS: *lavender, baby's breath, white geranium*
INCENSES: *lavender, jasmine, honeysuckle, heather*
OILS: *lavender, jasmine, honeysuckle, camphor*
CRYSTALS: *clear quartz, aragonite, lapis lazuli*
CANDLES: *white, lavender, pale blue, pale yellow*

Air Meditation

Relax and make yourself comfortable.

Take three slow, deep breaths. You are standing on an open cliff, overlooking a prairie below. It is shortly before dawn, and you have come here to do your magical work.

The sky is muted, pale blue overhead fading into a gentle dusty rose near the eastern horizon where the sun will rise. Relax as you stand on the cliff, watching the sky. Wisps of clouds drift by, strings of gray stretching across the horizon. They are distant and lazy and will burn off by morning.

Long Pause

The air currents are still in the chill, soon-to-warm morning, and your breath steams out, hovering in front of you just for a moment before it disappears. Now step to the edge of the cliff and stretch your hands out to the sky. In a voice that echoes across the valley, call out:

"Eurus, Wind of the East! Dazzling and bright! Aid me in my magical journey!"

As the last echo fades away, you see a huge bird winging toward you. It is a giant red-tailed hawk, and it soars in to land on the cliff next to you.

"Climb aboard my back. I will take you to Eurus," she says, and you straddle her behind her wings and hold on to the lavender straps that will give you balance. She crouches, then takes to the air. Your weight seems to present no problems, and you find yourself flying far overhead the cliff and the valley below.

Long Pause

The hawk climbs higher and higher, and you soon lose track of the ground altogether. After a while, the hawk heads for a cloud formation, soft strings drifting across the sky, which is the color of a robin's egg. Finally she lands on the edge of one. "Here is where you get off," she says. "Don't worry, the clouds will hold your weight."

You climb off of the hawk's back and find the clouds soft but substantial beneath your feet. The hawk flies away and, in another moment, she is a small speck in the sky.

You hear laughter in the distance, growing closer. A being of air sweeps up. The cool, crisp breezes of morning accompany him and he laughs again, and each breath washes you clean of cobwebs and stagnation.

Long Pause

"I am Eurus, Master of the Eastern Wind," he says. "Touch me and know my powers." Reach out and touch his hand.

As your fingers enter the wind stream around Eurus, you find your mind growing alert, aware. You feel clearheaded, and your thoughts come rapidly and coherently. Everything seems brighter, smells cleaner, and now the breeze rushes through your aura, cleaning away the stagnant energy that has accumulated there. A rush of exhilaration snaps you to attention.

Long Pause

"You see," he says, "my winds have the power to purify you, to free you from old habits. I am the wind of new beginnings. I am quicksilver, the wind of thought and communication. In my presence you will never be at a loss for words." Then Eurus gives you a feather. It is from the hawk. "Whenever you have need of my powers, use this feather to call them forth. Or call on the hawk to bring the east winds. And now," he says, "the next step of your journey awaits." With a rush, Eurus departs.

Long Pause

You tuck the feather away and turn to the edge of the cloud. You raise your hands to your mouth and call out into the clear blue sky, "Notus, Wind of the South! Fiery and radiant! Aid me in my magical journey!" As you wait, you see a winged creature approaching. It is not the hawk, but a gigantic bird covered in flames, golden and orange and brilliant red. A phoenix, and it lands beside you.

"Climb on my back, and I will take you to Notus," she says. You approach her, expecting to feel an intense heat radiating from her body, but instead, only a gentle warmth seeps through to you. You are protected from her fire by the Gods who sent her. Climb aboard her back and take hold of the golden straps and hold on tight.

Long Pause

She takes flight, and you soar through the air, rising toward another cloud. This cloud is huge and white, puffed cotton grown thoroughly wild. The phoenix lands carefully on the edge and allows you to dismount, then flies off again, a brilliant fireball in the sky.

You stand but a moment when you hear a laughter like thunder, a huge bellowing chuckle. The being that approaches comes in a hot, crackling wind and you feel the hairs on your arms rise, caught in static electricity.

Long Pause

"Welcome to the home of Notus," he says, and his voice echoes across the plain. "Feel my power and understand my radiance!"

You reach out to touch the energy of the Master of the South Wind. As your fingers meet his, the wind sweeps down around you and crackles, electricity at its strongest. You feel your mind leap with passion, the passion to act and to create. Stories, poems . . . pictures, they are all grounded here. You feel words swirling around you, just waiting for you to invoke them. Your body shivers; this wind is sensuous and plays gently, caressing and teasing you like hundreds of fingers tracing out patterns on your skin.

Long Pause

"You see," says Notus, "I am the winds of creativity, the wind that brings you the scent of new-mown hay where you lie down in passion with your love. I am the wind that precedes lightning." Then he gives you a feather from the phoenix. "Whenever you have need of my powers, use this feather to call me forth, or call on the phoenix to bring the southern winds. Now, the next step of your journey awaits!" And with a rush, Notus departs.

Long Pause

You go to the edge of the cloud and call out, "Zephyrus, Wind of the West! Gentle and buoyant! Aid me in my magical journey!" Watching, you see a winged creature approach. It is a great blue heron, and it lands beside you.

"I will take you to Zephyrus," she says softly, and you climb aboard and grab hold of the blue straps and find yourself once more aloft.

Long Pause

The heron brings you to a cloud that is darker than the others. It rolls across the sky at twilight, hinting of rain, black and full of moisture. As the heron lands, you climb off, and it flies away, leaving you alone.

You do not have to wait long. Soon another wind spirit rumbles up to meet you. His face is mournful. He does not laugh but remains melancholy, yet seems at peace with himself and the world.

Long Pause

"I am Zephyrus," he says, "Master of the West Wind. I bid you feel my powers and stay as long as you need."

You reach out and are swept into the storm. The rain pounds around you; this wind is full of moisture and blows cool against your skin. It whispers of peace in thought and action, of turning inward to look at yourself. It blows through your life and cleanses you of old wounds. It brings the rains of autumn to clear the air and make way for the frost.

Long Pause

"Behold," he says, "I am Zephyrus, and I bring to you the joys and sadness of the heart. I blow into your life when the mists are needed to cushion you, and I bring the fog to protect you from sight. I am the wind of autumn and of the beautiful sunset when the air is cool, when birds wing gently home. I bring fertility and respite."

He hands you a feather from the heron. "Use this when you have need of my powers, or call on the heron to bring you the west winds. Now, the next step of your journey awaits you." He drifts off, leaving you alone.

Long Pause

Once again you stand on the edge of the cloud and raise your hands to your mouth. "Boreas, Wind of the North! Rushing and mighty! Aid me in my magical journey!"

As your call goes ringing out, you see a bird gliding toward you. It is a giant eagle, and she lands and waits for you to climb aboard her back. The straps you take hold of are black. She rises silently, and you know she is taking you to the realm of Boreas, Master of the North Wind.

This cloud is gray, sparkling with frost, and you land silently, muffled. The eagle rises and leaves you with no words. A bitter chill sweeps down as the wind whirls up around you, swirling with snowflakes, and Boreas, Master of the North Wind, stands gravely before you.

Long Pause

"Behold, I am Boreas, Master of the North Wind. I welcome you and extend to you the knowledge of my realm." His wind comes sweeping around you, a howling gale of ferocity that brings with it deep snows and death and the darkness of winter's night.

Long Pause

"I am Boreas, and I bring with me sleep, the winds that clear the trees of their leaves, the wind that cries out, destroying old patterns and habits that lie in my path. I clear depression and anxiety and envy from your heart, leaving a void to be filled by the East Wind. Know that without me, there would be no beginning, for there must be an end to all things before new life can take hold. I guard the road of the dead, and ghosts live in my cry, and old memories; leave them to me, free yourself of your chains. I will sweep them up.

Long Pause

"And now," he says, handing you an eagle feather, "you must attend the last stage of your journey. Use this feather to call me, or bid the eagle to bring you the North Wind. But be aware, I will most surely come." Sparkling with frost, Boreas glides off in the muffled night.

Long Pause

You stand on the edge of the cloud and realize you have made the circuit of the four directions, leaving only the center. As you watch, a winged horse comes flying up and you climb aboard Pegasus's back. He carries you aloft, far higher than you have ever been. You are dizzy with the flight, spinning and whirling in the air.

Long Pause

You find yourself on the edge of a rainbow, and Pegasus bids you dismount. As you do so, you hear a sweet singing, chimes in the wind, and you turn to see a woman dressed in hues of pale blue and lavender, with golden threads woven through the silken veils. She wears a necklace of diamonds, and her hair is pulled back in a tight chignon, covered with a net of spider's web to keep it neat.

Long Pause

"Welcome," she says, and her voice is the echo of spring, the call of early morning. "Welcome to the realm of the Queen of Air."

She invites you to sit on the rainbow bridge and sits beside you, a bouquet of white daisies in her hand. "You have journeyed far to learn of my element, and so I will tell you of the nature of Air, element of the East. Know this: Without air, there is no life. Without my breath, you cease to exist. Without me, this world would be but a lifeless orb floating in space. I am essential, as are all elements, for survival.

"I am mist and fog, vapors trailing in the wind. I am the wind and the breeze, the still currents of air on a hot summer's night. Without me, fire would not exist, the earth would bear no life, and the water could support no fish."

Long Pause

Then the Queen of Air looks at you and says, "What would you ask of me? What do you need from me?"

Think carefully, then ask of her and listen for her reply.

Extended Long Pause—about two minutes

When she has spoken, she reaches out and helps you to your feet, and you feel the cool promise of morning beckoning you to rise from the bed for a new day awaits. "Slide down the rainbow," she says. "It will take you home, safely and quickly."

And then she is gone.

You look at the rainbow. It is steep but very wide, and when you sit down on it, you find there is no way you can fall off. You push off with your hands and find yourself speeding down the arc, watching the sky curve as you descend.

Long Pause

You breathe deeply, calming yourself, for you are traveling at a speed faster than thought. And you begin to count . . . each beat bringing you closer to the earth below.

Twenty . . . nineteen . . . eighteen . . . seventeen . . . you see clouds now, they slip past as you go racing by . . . sixteen . . . fifteen . . . fourteen . . . thirteen . . . twelve . . . and your speed begins to slow somewhat . . . eleven . . . ten . . . nine . . . you can see the rainbow curving toward the earth below . . . eight . . . you can see the tops of the trees and you slow even more . . . seven . . . six . . . five . . . four . . . you see the cliff on which you originally stood . . . three . . . two . . . you are almost to the bottom of the rainbow . . . one. You slide to the ground and turn, and the rainbow fades in the early morning. The sun is rising in the east. Welcome the new day. Take three deep breaths, and when you are ready, you may open your eyes.

Suggested Exercises for Air Meditation

1. Spend some time outdoors each day for the next week, focusing on the air and wind currents.
2. Practice the *Listening to Breath Exercise* twice each day.
3. Spend time bird-watching, noticing in particular how birds react to being on the ground.
4. Spend some time each day for the next week actively reading and analyzing what you read.
5. Gather together four feathers, one representing each of the four winds, and use them in your magic when you call the element of Air, matching the type of spell you are casting. Some suggestions:

NORTH: *raven, crow, myna*
EAST: *peacock, owl, robin*
SOUTH: *parrot, macaw, cardinal*
WEST: *goose, duck, grouse*

Fire

The third part of our elemental journey leads us to the south, the home of Fire. There are several aspects to Fire: faerie fire, flame, the sun, bonfires, and lava to name a few.

The element of Fire encompasses passion, creativity, transmutation, playfulness, vitality, and healing. When touched by Fire, form changes and alters. Fire is transformative.

Fire is associated with the south, midday, and the summer months.

Guidelines for Use

This meditation is appropriate whenever you need change. Be aware that Fire changes things quickly; it moves swiftly. Therefore, be cautious when working with Fire. Don't apply excessive force when using this element because the results can be anything from fiery transformation at best, to chaotic mayhem and destruction at worst. I suggest that you use this meditation when you are striving for a breakthrough on the creative level or when you are feeling a need for more energy, vitality, or passion in your life.

I recommend keeping the room quite warm during this meditation. Use the *Loosening the Body Exercise* before you begin.

FLOWERS: *red carnation, sunflower, marigold*

INCENSES: *carnation, cinnamon, tangerine, spice*

OILS: *carnation, orange, tangerine, lime*

CRYSTALS: *carnelian, peridot, garnet, copper, sulfur*

CANDLES: *red, orange, gold, peridot, yellow*

Fire Meditation

Relax and make yourself comfortable.

Close your eyes and take three deep breaths.

You have traveled far, through land and air, to search for the realm of Fire. Now you find yourself standing on a dusty road. Up ahead, you see a copse of trees, tall and dark. It is near midnight, and there is little light from the waning moon to guide your journey.

The path leads to the grove. The night is warm, and the gentle breeze carries the lingering heat of the day.

The trees are mingled oak and cedar and alder. Here and there a rowan hangs heavy with berries, and holly peeks out of the corners. As you enter the forest, a strange tingle runs up and down your arms, and you suddenly feel drowsy. All of your senses are on alert, yet you feel as if something has taken hold of your conscious mind and is lulling you into a hazy, drifting fog. But you feel no sense of fear, no sense of danger, only a sense of great powers watching you.

Long Pause

You pass through the wood, quietly now, drifting along the path. Every sound seems heightened; every movement catches your attention, and you realize that you could pass through this wood blindfolded if you had to.

As you continue on your journey, you see a deer flit into the undergrowth, and an owl swoops down and passes you overhead. Then you feel someone following you, and you stop and turn around. Behind you, you see a ball of light, glowing with green energy the color of peridot, floating gently in midair.

Long Pause

"I am to be your guide in this part of the realm of Fire." The voice echoes inside your head, and you know it's from the globe of light. "I am a will-o'-the-wisp, and I belong to the realm of faerie fire, through which you first must pass. Follow me then, to the grotto ahead, and do not tarry, for the realm of faerie is quick to catch the unwary and the foolish in its snares and weavings."

You follow the will-o'-the-wisp as it leads the way through the forest.

Long Pause

Now you begin to notice a shimmering on the trees, their auras glowing and sparkling bright. "This has always been; you can only now perceive it," says the globe. "Your first stop is over to your left."

Just up ahead, to your left, you see a darkened patch in the foliage. As you near it, a shiver runs through your body and your mind quakes, for there is a stirring of power around you, and you know something very ancient, very primal, is there. You creep forward and turn to gaze in the dark space between the trees.

Long Pause

The blackness is the color of the abyss, the darkness of the void, and it holds your gaze, hypnotizing you with its incredible depths. Then, just as you think you can't stand gazing into the emptiness any longer, you begin to see a swirl of sparkling color, a spiral, and the spiral forms itself into two glowing red eyes that pierce the abyss far better than any lantern or torch.

The gaze of the red eyes strips away your outer facades and masks, delving into the inner self you keep hidden away. It is not malevolent, but strong and male and watchful.

Long Pause

"The red eyes in the forest at midnight," whispers the globe of light. "The Hunter, the Heart of the Forest, he exists in the realm of faerie fire. Watch your step and mind your actions when crossing the woods at night, for he will be there watching you."

Quietly, ask the Hunter what he has to teach you about fire, and listen well for his reply.

Long Pause

"Now follow me," says the will-o'-the-wisp, and you pass through the forest, listening to the calls of the birds. Up ahead, the path diverges to the right, and the will-o'-the-wisp detours, floating along that fork in the road. Follow, but be careful here, for the slope is steep, leading to a beach down below. When you have walked and slid your way down to the sand, you find yourself on the shores of a small bay that kisses the shore. The water is shimmering with lights, green and blue and pink and yellow.

Overcome with a rush of delight, you dash forward, drawn in by the glittering lights. With every step, sparks fly from the sand, and you stop to press your hands on the ground. When you lift them, they are covered with sparkles. Suddenly lighthearted, laughing and unable to speak, for the joy in your heart is overwhelming any words you might have to say, you dance on the sand and watch the sparks fly. If you like, wade into the water, where the sparkles glitter around you and it feels like you're wading among the stars.

Long Pause

Finally the will-o'-the-wisp speaks, and it says, "You see, faerie fire is an inexplicable feeling. There are few words to encompass the depths of this happiness, this intoxication, but it exists and is real. Now come, back to the path, for I have one more stop to show you, and then you will go forward without me."

As you return to the path, you find your clothes are dry, but the phosphorescent sparkles of faerie fire still exist within your heart and memory. The will-o'-the-wisp guides you along the path until, up ahead, you see a purple fire dancing across the road. You must pass through it to continue your journey.

"Go now," the globe says, "and when you pass through the fire of the phoenix, you will find a fine layer of ash covering your body. The wind will blow it away, and with it will go pain and anger and old bonds that chain you. The purple rays of the phoenix are hotter than flame, hotter than fire, and they will burn through to your core and leave you purified and new, ready for the next stage of your journey. After you have passed through it, you will find yourself at the end of the forest, near a green fire that covers the road. This flame is the purest essence of faerie fire, and you must pass through it before journeying on the next leg of your quest. Good luck, and good-bye." And the will-o'-the-wisp fades into the forest.

You approach the flickering purple flame; the heat is intense, almost violent, but it gives off no actual warmth, only waves of energy that ripple through your body and soul. Take a moment, think of what you would have burned away from you, what you are tired of carrying around, and then pass into the flame, bathe in it, and come out the other side.

Extended Long Pause—about one minute

When you emerge from the phoenix flame, a fine layer of ash covers your body. The breeze sweeps up and blows it away. Beneath the ash, your skin is new and clear, and your heart feels lighter.

The forest comes to an end up ahead, and there you find the green flame waiting. Take one last look behind you, and then pass into the flame of faerie fire, the green fire in the forest at midnight, the green fire of Midsummer's Eve.

It crackles around you, sparkling and magnetic. It resonates within you as your aura shifts and changes. You move with more grace in the fire, as it slides up your arms and legs, seeping into your belly; sensuous, it leaves you breathless and waiting.

Long Pause

Now you find you can shape your aura; you can change and alter it to your liking. Do you want to appear taller? Thinner? More voluptuous? Do you want to radiate confidence and strength? All you have to do is use the faerie fire to shape your will. When you have thought and done your workings, step through to the other side and look at yourself again to see what changes you have made in your energy.

Extended Long Pause—about one minute

Now step out of the forest and look around. You are standing at the edge of an open plain. The grass is thick here, but grows sparse up ahead, and you see the light of dawn rising to the east. There are no trees after the line of the forest, and the path slopes upward, a gently graded incline. Follow the path and continue your journey as the morning light grows and the stars fade from the sky.

It looks like the morning is going to be hot. There are no clouds in the sky, and the forest has become a distant memory. The path seems long and dusty, and up ahead you see a well. A sign on it reads, Last Water for Many Miles. There are canteens here, and you might want to fill one, for the journey is sure to be hot and thirsty.

Long Pause

The grass is sparse now, the dirt faded and compacted. Cracks fracture the ground; no rain has fallen here for a long time. The sun has now risen above the horizon, and you are already starting to sweat.

Wipe your forehead and look around. In all directions it seems there is only the desert, with occasional outcroppings of stone. As you set out again, your feet become hot and weary, and after a while they feel like they're beginning to blister. A large rock to the side of the road offers you a seat, and you find it surprisingly comfortable when you sit down to rest. As you take your break, a rustle to your left alerts you. Look down to the left side of the rock.

A large lizard is sitting there, patiently watching you.

Long Pause

Red with stripes of orange, the lizard's golden eyes stare up at you. Its long tongue forks out, and it says in a wheezing, whistling voice, "I'm your guide for this part of the journey. I am the salamander Flametongue. I will guide you to your destination in this part of the realm of fire. You will need a walking stick. Look under that rock over there." It waves its tongue toward a low, long rock near you, and underneath it you find a walking stick that's just the right height for you.

Long Pause

"Well, then," Flametongue says, "it's time we were off. Come now; follow me." The salamander leads you up the path, which has become much steeper. As you climb the path, your muscles ache and burn, but you know that you cannot tarry; there are important lessons waiting up ahead. Finally, when you think you can't go any farther, you reach the top and see a cone-shaped mountain ahead. Dark, with streaks of rust-colored rocks trailing down its side, the mountain is formed of blackened lava that flowed out of its cone to cover the land long ago.

The hardened lava lies in waves, pillows of rock, thick and glistening with volcanic glass. Strange configurations, some looking almost human, stand frozen over the land. The ancient flow goes on for miles and miles, so vast that you can only imagine what it must have looked like when it first covered the land.

Long Pause

As you start forward, you find that the path no longer exists. You must cross the hardened lava, so, using your walking stick to steady yourself, you forge ahead, slowly working your way around the twisted rock. You must be careful here, for the lava is sharp and full of rough edges. If you fall, you could hurt yourself.

Flametongue leads you along the surface of the jagged rock. Your feet slide along the smooth obsidian rock. It is difficult to keep your balance here. At one point, your stick breaks through the lava, and you see the end of it smoke as it touches still-cooling rock. You pull it out quickly and beat out the flicker of flame that starts on its tip.

Long Pause

The salamander leads you a wide berth around that area, and you find yourself having to really concentrate to keep your footing as you realize how dangerous this realm can be.

Now the grade is rough, and you are breathing heavily. The taste of sulfur fills your mouth, and you must stop and pour a little water on your handkerchief. Tie the bandana around your face so the bitter, sulfuric fumes don't overwhelm you.

As you climb higher and higher up the side of the mountain, steam rises from cracks in the lava around you. Flametongue turns and says, "This is a place of massive destruction. But out of that destruction, new land is born; nutrients will weather down and feed the soil, and plants will grow again."

You curve around the side of the mountain; when you look over the edge of the roughly worn path, you see a drop, two hundred feet down, into a lake of lava. The lava boils and turns, and twisting red tongues of flame dance on its surface. At once terrifying and mesmerizing, it churns constantly as you watch.

Long Pause

"Come," says the salamander, "we shouldn't linger here. The Queen of Fire awaits you, and it's not wise to anger her."

The path twists away from the lake of magma and curves around the blackened mountain. You pass into what once was a forest. The trees are now blackened—hardened charcoal; they protrude out of the knee-deep ash that covers the land. The salamander leads you off the lava, and you sift your way through the ash into the desolate forest, where ghostly voices travel on the hot wind.

"The blade of fire is a double-edged sword," says Flametongue. "At its most constructive, the flames burn brightly; they drive us onward and fuel our creative and passionate selves. But when they turn to destruction, fire consumes all in its path, leaving only the ashes of history behind. Never underestimate the power of the flames; what might seem like a single spark can flare up into a raging inferno if the energy is not directed, focused, and given boundaries."

Your throat is parched, so stop and drink from your canteen. Your skin is drying out from the heat, and you desperately wish for a cool bath, somewhere very far away from this eternal land of heat and fire.

Long Pause

"We're almost there," says the salamander. "Can you see it up ahead—the home of the Queen of Fire?"

And indeed, when you shade your eyes against the sun and look, you see a great fountain, carved from blocks of frozen lava, sitting in a clearing full of ash. It is a fountain of flame and incandescent heat, and in the center of the flame, a woman bathes. Her skin is of purest crimson, her hair streaming vermilion, and her eyes mirror the brilliance of the sun. Surely, her gaze will blind you if you meet it directly. She motions you to come near.

Long Pause

As you approach, the heat intensifies until it feels like tiny blisters are about to bubble up on your skin. The woman holds up her hand for you to stop, and in a voice low and crackling, throaty with passion, she says, "Come no farther or my flames will harm you. I am the Queen of Fire. Welcome to my realm."

Sensuous, her body shifts shape in the flame, and the passion that throbs just below the surface of her element reaches out to encompass you. She speaks again. "Hold out your hand, so you may feel my power."

At first, you feel a warm glow—the warmth of spring mornings, the warmth of a breezy day when you're in the garden. Then the warmth increases and becomes the heat of the woodstove, warming you on crisp autumn evenings . . . the heat changes again, and it's the crackle of bonfires and the smell of burning wood . . . then once again, and the heat is the sweltering heat of noon on a summer's day, and sweat pours down your face.

Long Pause

"I am the drive of passion," the Queen of Fire says. "And I am the creative force that refuses to be squelched. Try to repress me, and I will rise up and burn you to ashes. Embrace me, use me with foresight, and I am an ally you cannot afford to lose. I heal with my golden rays, and with my rivers of molten rock that pour from the womb of the earth, I destroy. My destruction makes way for new creation, and this cycle has repeated itself from the beginning of time. Now what would you have me do for you? What do you wish to create? Tell me, and then listen and I will give you advice."

Think now for a moment, then answer and listen for her reply.

Extended Long Pause—about two minutes

When she has spoken, the Queen of Fire bids you leave. "This is not a place where mortals may stay for long. The heat will burn you ragged. Go now; there is a path beyond this fountain. Follow it and it will lead you home."

You follow the path, and it leads you down a slope. The sun is now a bit lower in the sky, and the salamander bids you good-bye. The walking becomes a little easier, the ash thins out, and you see fewer and fewer of the stunted trees.

As you proceed down the hill, wisps of grass begin to peek through the soil. Follow the open path by a low cliff and, looking beyond, you see the path leads to the shore below.

Long Pause

You twist and turn, going down, and find the walking easy and pleasant after your sojourn in the realm of Fire. When you reach the shoreline, you find a horse waiting, saddled.

Before you mount the horse, wade into the surf and wash the ash and soot from your body, luxuriating in the cool cleansing powers of the water. Then, when you are refreshed, settle yourself in the saddle. The horse seems to sense your exhaustion, so it follows its sense of internal direction and you find you can rest.

You ride for what seems like hours, and then the horse takes a fork that leads away from the water, and you find yourself traveling through late evening on a path that is gradually ascending a hill. At the top of the slope, just before twilight, the horse stops and you climb off. You see, ten steps in front of you, the place where you began your journey. The horse has brought you back to your path along your journey.

Long Pause

Now, take those twenty steps and each one, as I count, will bring you toward waking consciousness. Twenty . . . nineteen . . . eighteen . . . seventeen . . . you are becoming more alert . . . sixteen . . . fifteen . . . fourteen . . . thirteen . . . the sounds around you are becoming clearer . . . twelve . . . eleven . . . ten . . . nine . . . you are becoming aware of the world around you . . . eight . . . seven . . . six . . . five . . . four . . . you will awake clear and refreshed . . . three . . . two . . . one . . . take three deep breaths, and when you are ready, you may open your eyes.

Suggested Exercises for Fire Meditation

1. After the meditation do some ecstatic dancing or drumming (I suggest the music of Gabrielle Roth or Dead Can Dance) to utilize the energy raised; it's hard to shake Fire once you build it in your system. When you dance, always have a focus in mind for the energy so it doesn't fly off and create chaos. Before you begin to dance, think of a goal (for example, exercising regularly) or a focus (for example, an empowerment charm you recently made). As you dance, let the music move your body, and keep that goal or focus in mind. As the energy builds while you are dancing, mentally charge the goal or focus. When the energy has built to the point where you must release it, bathe your goal or focus with the power as it drains from your body. After you have finished dancing, always ground and center.

2. For the week following your meditation, pay attention to candle flame, bonfires, the fire in your woodstove, the heat from the electric baseboards, the warm air coming from your blow-dryer, the sunlight. Get to know the different aspects of Fire.

3. Think about changes you would like to make in the creative or physical aspects of your life. What can you do to make those changes? Are they realistic changes for you to work toward?

Water

We have come to the last leg of our journey through the elements. We have grounded ourselves in the earth, soared on the winds, and walked through the fire. Now we must turn to the west. Here we will dive into the depths of the ocean, allowing the element of Water to pour through our lives.

The element of Water encompasses emotions and feelings, cleansing, intuition, and the hidden depths of the psyche. It is associated with the autumn months and with twilight.

Guidelines for Use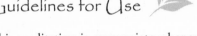

This meditation is appropriate whenever you are healing from an emotional trauma. It is useful for discovering your true feelings about an issue, and I recommend using it whenever you want to get in touch with your psychic self.

Since this meditation focuses so intensely on the emotions, it might bring up old issues with which you need to make peace. If you find it difficult to resolve these issues, especially if they are highly sensitive, you might find it helpful to talk to a qualified therapist or counselor. There are many good doctors, and there's no shame or embarrassment in admitting you need some help. Most cities have Crisis Lines and Women's Crisis Lines. These can be invaluable resources.

Take a warm bath with bath salts or bubble bath to enhance this meditation.

PLANTS: *iris, pink rose, lily, lilac*
INCENSES: *rose, lilac, honeysuckle, heather*
OILS: *rose, lilac, honeysuckle, heather, lemon*
CRYSTALS: *amethyst, rose quartz, fluorite, aquamarine*
CANDLES: *blue, white, sea green*

Water Meditation

Relax and make yourself comfortable.

Close your eyes and take three deep breaths.

You have searched through the elements—through Earth, Air, and Fire—and now you come to the last quarter in the Wheel. You are on a quest to explore the element of Water.

You begin your journey on an overcast day, near a forest of deep, dark coniferous woods, where rumor has it that somewhere within exists a beautiful grotto. A wide stream runs into the wood, and you stand on its bank, looking down into the ravine shaded by fern and long, dripping moss that beards the trees.

Turn to the wood and begin your journey, traveling alongside the stream bank. There is no well-worn path here; you have to climb over fallen logs covered with moss and skirt large chunks of granite deposited here during the last march of the glaciers.

As you enter the wood, the heavy growth dampens the glow from the sun as day fades toward the horizon. The sound of birds echoes around you, and a tinge of autumn chill drifts in the air, hints of cold nights to come. The stream gushes along beside you. At first the ravine is steep, and you cannot feel the spray of the water as it rushes past. Gradually the slope of the wood lowers to where you are only a few feet above the streambed, and you can see clearly below the surface of the water if you bend down.

Long Pause

Water skimmers dart across the surface of the bubbling water, and a few mosquitoes drone over the tide pools. Small fish flicker just below the surface—quicksilver, almost as if they aren't even there.

You find the walking easy at first, and the continual susurration of the water lulls you as you travel. It's cool near the stream, in fact it's almost chilly, and sometimes as you walk along you can hear a late-season frog croaking. The forest thickens, but you have become focused on the stream below. Occasionally laughter rises from the water, but you can't see who it's coming from.

The current picks up, and you feel a sense of urgency now, inspired by the force of the water. You begin walking faster, trying to keep up with the ever-running stream. And then, up ahead, you see that a large cliff blocks the path, making it impossible to continue on the stream banks. You could go around it, but you'd lose sight of the stream, and by now you know that you're on the right path to find the grotto. But there is one other option. You could let the stream carry you along; it's deep and swift now. So you step forward and jump into the water.

Long Pause

The first shock of chill water stuns you, and you flounder for a moment, fighting the current that drags you past the cliffs. You manage to catch your breath and straighten out, riding the current on your tummy. You don't have to swim; just stretch out and let the waves buoy you up.

Now the last shadows of daylight are glistening on the water around you. It sparkles like brilliant sapphire, dazzling your eyes. You're soaked, but find yourself adapting to the waterborne journey; it's easier to remain calm now, easier to stretch your arms out in front of you and steer yourself around the occasional rock jutting up from the water.

The pulse of the current begins to match your heartbeat as a strong quiver runs through the water. With each breath you take, the stream seems to rise. Every time you exhale, the stream lowers, and you gently but swiftly flow along, almost as if you were a part of the water itself.

Long Pause

The cliffs through which you pass are steep and dark, towering blocks of granite, and there is no turning back. You have no choice except to let the water be your guide. Suddenly thirsty, you open your lips and let a mouthful of water slide down your throat. The icy glacier water refreshes you like no other drink ever before.

A roaring sound echoes up ahead, and again the water picks up speed. You raise your head to try and see what's coming, but it's difficult to see much from this position. Suddenly, you find yourself teetering on the edge of a waterfall, with no handholds in sight. All you have time for is a glimpse of white water mist spraying all around you before you plunge over the edge.

Long Pause

Twisting and turning, you manage to right yourself and find that you're actually sliding down the falls, buoyed by the force of the cascading water. You catch a glimpse of a glistening pool below, and fern-covered slopes surrounding it, then hit the surface and sink.

Every time you try to swim upward, kicking and fighting all the way, you manage to grab another breath, then once again you are pulled beneath the surface. You're spinning now, and each time you break the surface, you gain a breath of air, but it's hard to pull free from the whirlpool you're caught in.

The water circles around you, tearing at your clothes, stripping away any possessions you might be carrying. When you think you've reached your last gasp, you manage one final kick and push yourself out of the vortex to a place where you can navigate away from the whirlpool. With this last bit of energy, you swim to shore and crawl onto the sand. You find you're naked; your clothes have been swept away, and all possessions you had with you are gone. You're so tired, you just sit and rest.

Long Pause

As you regain your strength, the cold begins to seep into your bones. Your skin is dry, but the night air is so cool you begin to shiver. You must reach shelter soon before you freeze. Wearily drag yourself to your feet and look around for anything that might help.

The dusk is thick, but you see a line of dark caves against the ravine walls, and you imagine there might be a few below the surface as well. Fern and moss grow along the sides of the cliff, and willows surround the pool. Could this be the grotto? No, a little voice inside whispers; you haven't found it yet.

A thick, long drape of moss is hanging from the cliff side nearest you, and the thought occurs that this velvety cloak might provide some protection from the cold. Pull it down from the rock wall and wrap it around you, tucking it in so it makes a kind of sarong. Surprisingly, the moss robe helps to break the chill. Look around some more; the fern fronds are long enough to weave into a kind of cloak. Gather a few and weave them into a makeshift cape to drape around your shoulders; when you finish and try it on, you find that you feel comfortable enough to notice how hungry you are.

Movement on the beach catches your eye. An otter has come out of the pool and is staring at you. She's got something in her mouth. You take a step closer, not wanting to spook her, but she remains calm, and when you are almost within range to reach out and touch her, she drops a fish at your feet.

"Your dinner," a voice in your head rings out, and then you hear laughter similar to the laughter you heard earlier, in the stream. Her voice is playful, and she waits for you to pick up the fish.

Long Pause

When you do, you find the fish is dead, and she's sliced it open with her claws and washed it in the pool. There's no fire, but the water here is clean and clear, and you know the fish is safe to eat. Bite into the flesh. It's juicy and sweet, and your stomach gurgles with the promise of a meal. As you eat the fish, you can feel its life force streaming into your body; you feel shimmering and sleek, and energy races through your blood.

Thank the fish for its life, for sustaining you, and then turn back to the otter.

Long Pause

She smiles, her whiskers sticking out, and then she says, "When you've rested, you must climb through that cave if you want to reach the grotto." Then, quick as a wink, she slides back in the pool and disappears under the water. You feel energetic now, strong and ready to continue, so you carefully climb over the rocks and up to the dark slit that awaits.

The cavern is narrow and high. You feel your way along, running your hand over one of the walls. Before long, it opens out into a mammoth room with stalagmites and stalactites glistening from a phosphorescent glow. There are no other entrances or exits, but in the center of the room you see a large pool. The water in the pool is black and filled with twinkling light.

You hear singing rising from that pool, indescribably sweet and alluring. The voices echo and rebound off the walls, and your heart begins to pound as you're overcome by the desire to follow the voices.

They swirl around you, reverberating in your mind, and they sing, "Come to us, come to us, leave your home, leave your loves, leave your families and ride with us into the sea." The pull is so strong that, try as you might, you can't escape and so plunge into the pool, searching for the singers of that melody.

Long Pause

As you sink into the water, something begins to happen. You feel strange, your body is shifting, altering. You find yourself changing into a creature of the sea, perhaps a salmon, an otter, a trout, an octopus. Look at your body, and find out what you've transformed into. Feel the fins, tentacles; feel the way the water moves around you now that you don't have to fight to breathe. Play with your transformation for a moment.

Long Pause

After you have gotten used to the idea that you're no longer human, you begin to swim deeper and deeper, following the current of the pool as it leads you down. Ahead of you, you see a tunnel in the water, a cave going underneath the cliff, and you follow it. You can still hear the voices singing, filtering through the tunnel.

As you swim through the darkened tube it grows lighter. Now you swim up and up, heading toward the surface. As you break the water's edge, you shift again and are back in your human form.

Long Pause

You are near the shore of a large lake, and the forest surrounding this lake shimmers and glows. As you head inland toward the shore, you're able to wade through the water. Crystals glisten in the sand, and the full moon hangs low overhead, casting its light across the grotto.

Stand on the shore, looking back at the lake to get an idea of where you are. The forest entirely surrounds the lake with a shimmering light. In the center of the lake is a large rock, and you know that's where the singing emanates from, and that's where you must go.

Long Pause

Plunge back into the water. This time, you remain your human self and, as you begin to swim out to the rock, you hope your strength will sustain you long enough to reach your destination.

The shore grows farther away behind you as the water ripples with gentle currents. They seem to help you along at first, guiding your way, holding you up. The lake lulls you into a bliss that you've never experienced before, surrounding and warming you. Flash back to the time when you lay in your mother's womb, where the amniotic fluid cushioned you against the hardships of the outer world. Take a moment to reexperience that cushioned rocking, and see what it means to you.

Long Pause

You are quite a distance from shore when the water begins to grow choppy. You shake out of that peaceful calm state as you realize that you must remain alert, watching as the water swells and crests, the waves growing larger. The going could be dangerous here, and your muscles begin to ache because you can't relax; you must be aware of your surroundings.

Now you are closing in on the rock, but the passage becomes more difficult. The waves grow dangerous; they tug at you, and you use all of your strength to fight the current in order to reach your goal. Rain begins to pelt down, stinging like hail as it drives into the surface of the water. The night is so cold now that your muscles are starting to cramp, but the rock is almost within reach.

Long Pause

The water swells again with a big wave coming in, but as it swells you reach out; and the current pushes you just far enough toward the rock to grab hold of an outcropping. Dig in your fingers and pull yourself to the granite, and then, with bleeding hands, the skin torn from small lacerations, drag yourself up onto the rock.

Rest for a moment.

Long Pause

You lie there for what seems like an interminable amount of time, but eventually you begin to catch your breath and when you sit up, you see you're not the only one on the rock. A ring of women, beautiful and so ethereal they almost seem formed of mist, surround you, singing. But now that you're here, their songs seem to have little effect on you.

In the center of their midst stands a great throne carved of mother-of-pearl and amethyst, and on the throne sits a woman cloaked in long streams of dripping seaweed. Her hair is the color of twilight, and she wears a gown woven of fog and raindrops. She sits in front of a large bowl, so large you could crawl into it, and the bowl is filled with a water darker than any you've ever seen.

Long Pause

She motions for you to come forward. When you are standing at her feet, she says, "I am Aqualia, the Queen of Cups, the Queen of Water. You have come to seek my element." Her voice echoes with the roar of the waterfall.

She continues, "Know this, I am the force of your body, I am the home from which life began. Your ancestors swam in my primordial seas. I cushion your tears and soothe you with my gentle raindrops. But I am also the force of the gale, the wild cresting waves, the roar of the hurricane, the encompassing floodwaters that rise without check. Do not underestimate me or deny my strength."

Long Pause

As she speaks, a great serpent rises from the water, greater than any serpent ever before known or seen. Aqualia says, "I am Tiamat, Primordial Mother of the Ocean. Know me and pay me respect."

Long Pause

Then she shifts again and stands cloaked in a golden girdle; she is the loveliest woman you've ever seen. "I am Aphrodite, the foam born. Love me and desire me and ride on my waves of passion."

Long Pause

Once more she shifts, and she is wild and fearsome and full of dark storm clouds. "I am Ran, goddess of the angry seas, and I drown sailors who dare to challenge my strength. Do not think you can best me. I am always more powerful than you."

Long Pause

Then she is back to herself again, and she sits down and smiles gently. "Know also, I'm in each raindrop that falls from the heavens, I'm in each teardrop you shed, and when you drink of me, you bring my life force into your body."

Long Pause

She points to the bowl in front of her. "I give you a gift. If you drink from my dark wine while asking a question, then close your eyes, you will hear the answer within your heart. For my waters unlock the gates to your subconscious; from there, spring the answers you seek." She hands you a crystal goblet and says, "Think of your need to know, then drink and listen." The water glistens as you stand before it. Now do as she bids and listen for the answer.

Extended Long Pause—about two minutes

When you have finished your task, she gives you the goblet to keep and says, "Place water that has been charged under the dark moon in this goblet, and you may touch the wells of knowledge by drinking deep." Then she says, "It is time for you to leave. You have followed the wheel of elements, and now you must blend them before you go on to your next journey, the journey within." As she speaks, a boat comes sailing to the rock, and she bids you board and sit tight.

The boat glides silently over the water to the other side of the shore, but before you reach the shore, a great mist rises, and you can no longer see anything beyond the fog. As you glide along in the vapors, the boat suddenly comes to a stop. The mist lifts just a little, and you see a staircase rising from the side of the boat. You can't see where it goes, but you know you must climb it. There are five stairs.

Long Pause

When you step on the first stair, you feel the earth groan and twist beneath you, and the energy from that element races through your body, leaving you rooted.

Long Pause

When you step on the second stair, you feel the air whip around you, and the energy from that element races through your mind, leaving you cleansed and alert.

Long Pause

When you step on the third stair, you feel the flames from the earth crackle around you, and the energy from that element races through your blood, leaving you impassioned and full of drive.

Long Pause

When you step on the fourth stair, you feel the waters rush around you, and the energy from that element races through your heart, leaving you hearing the voices of your subconscious.

Long Pause

When you step on the last stair, you find yourself balanced between light and dark, all elements mingling in your body.

Long Pause

Now, as I count from twenty to one, you will become awake and alert, and the feeling of balance will stay with you as you go about your daily life.

Twenty . . . nineteen . . . eighteen . . . seventeen . . . you are becoming more alert . . . sixteen . . . fifteen . . . fourteen . . . thirteen . . . the sounds around you are becoming clearer . . . twelve . . . eleven . . . ten . . . nine . . . you are becoming aware of the world around you . . . eight . . . seven . . . six . . . five . . . four . . . you will awake clear and refreshed . . . three . . . two . . . one . . . take three deep breaths, and when you are ready, you may open your eyes.

Suggested Exercises for Water Meditation

1. Gather water from different sources—a lake, a stream, the ocean, a tap, New Moon Water, and Full Moon Water (see appendix 2). Pour each into a separate bowl. Dip your hand in each bowl for a moment and close your eyes. What impressions do you get from each source of water? Do the waters feel the same, or are there differences in texture and energy?

2. Chart your moods during periods of dry weather and periods of rainy weather. How do they differ? Is there a regular pattern?

3. If your health permits, fast for one day, drinking only large quantities of lemon water. Then, in the evening, go through the *Water Meditation* and afterward the *Cleansing and Protecting Meditation.*

4. Spend time outdoors near an open body of water. Watch the currents, dip your feet in it, go swimming or wading. Get to know the natural flow of the water.

5. Visit a fish run at the nearest dam (if your area has one). You can also visit a public aquarium or an aquatic theme park. Or simply sit in front of a fish tank and watch the fish and how they move in response to their environment.

PART 3

Meditations on
the Sabbats

Notes for Readers and Guides:

Please read the sections on *How to Use This Book* and *Basics of Meditation* to get a thorough grounding in how to use these meditations.

- If you are guiding a meditation, be aware that certain thoughts can trigger extreme emotional responses. You should watch the group carefully as you lead the meditation. If someone appears distressed, ask them quietly whether they need assistance. Usually they will be able to work through the problem without your help, but it pays to be observant.

- If you are tape-recording these meditations or guiding a group, at the end of each paragraph pause for a slow, silent count of five seconds, then continue. Where I have indicated a long pause in the test, pause for approximately thirty seconds. This should give those meditating plenty of time to contemplate the thoughts presented.

As I have said, these meditations are essentially self-hypnosis and as such, it would be dangerous to drive right after you have finished. Take pains to include the last paragraph of each meditation, which should bring you out of trance. As an added suggestion, I recommend that, after practicing each meditation, you eat something light, preferably high in protein, to ground yourself in the mundane world once more.

Samhain

The first Sabbat of the cycle known as the Wheel of the Year, this holiday is celebrated by Wiccans and by a number of Witches and Pagans from many cultures. The Wheel of the Year holidays are celebrated under different names, but they have a common intent.

Samhain, pronounced *sow-een*, is celebrated on the first day of November. Samhain is considered the third harvest festival, or the meat harvest. Traditionally this was the time when animals were slaughtered for the year's meat supply and when much of the hunting was done.

Samhain is the Celtic festival of the dead. It is the time when the veil that separates the spirit world from that of mortals is at its thinnest. It is a time to remember our ancestors and to toast the dead. It is a celebration that is introspective and, usually, somber. There are many similar festivals around the world. In Finland, for example, the Kekri festival (also known as Keyri or Käyri) honored the ancestors, Día de los Muertos honors the dead in Mexico, and the Japanese Obon festival is a remembrance festival to honor the spirits.

Guidelines for Use

This meditation is appropriate for use either during a Samhain ritual or preceding it. I recommend incorporating it into a ritual.

Because of the active nature of this meditation, the guide should read through it several times. Before the meditation is presented, the guide should clarify to the group that there will be guided dancing in the middle of the meditation, and when the dancing is over the participants will return to their original positions. These active periods are noted in the text of the meditation. If a member of the group cannot take part in the actual dancing, they can journey along in their minds and adapt the activity to a level that is suitable to their abilities. If possible, it would be wonderful to have the dancing around a bonfire.

Because this meditation involves dancing, you should have music ready to play. It also involves the use of a drumbeat, which you might want to pre-record. If you are doing this in a group setting, the guide can work together with a drummer before the actual meditation to coordinate the words and the beat. I recommend music by Gabrielle Roth or Dead Can Dance or similar music for the dancing. As an added precaution, if you are using a battery-operated cassette player, make sure your batteries are in good working order. If there will be live drummers, the guide should tell them in advance what they are expected to play and when.

Each person should bring a pumpkin to the meditation, and they should have carved it to match the totem animal with which they intend to work. Candles should be lit within the pumpkins during the meditation, and each person should keep their pumpkin nearby so they can focus on it during the meditation. If you are practicing this meditation at a time when pumpkins are out of season or in an area where they don't grow, you can use any round root vegetable as a substitute. Or you can carve your totem animal on an orange or brown pumpkin- or ball-shaped candle and then light the candle itself.

PLANTS:	*dried statice, chrysanthemum, white rose*
INCENSES:	*copal, musk, spice, patchouli, kyphi*
OILS:	*musk, sandalwood, patchouli*
CRYSTALS:	*carnelian, bloodstone, jasper*
CANDLES:	*black, white, orange, brown, skull candles, pumpkin-shaped candles*

Samhain Totem Animal Meditation

Relax and make yourself comfortable.

Set your pumpkin so that it is facing you.

Take three deep breaths. Let the tensions of the week pass out of your body and drain away into the void, where they will be transformed and cleansed.

Long Pause

Now, focus your attention on the stem area of your gourd. See the light emanating from the face you've carved in the pumpkin. Spend a few moments letting the animal essence come to the surface; look at it, get to know it, let it enter your psyche.

Long Pause

Know that it is Samhain Eve, and we are here, as so many have come before, with the dead walking beside us and the Gods standing at our shoulders.

We gather to pay our respects to those we've loved and lost, knowing they are gone but not forgotten. We gather to remember the journey that the Horned Lord makes into the Halls of the Underworld to meet the Crone, who sacrificed him at Lughnasadh.

We gather to acknowledge the unalterable power of death, to respect its place in the eternal turning of the Cycle. Our ancestors knew this, and we know this, so we gather to celebrate Samhain, the Day of the Dead.

This day, all veils are thin, and so we make other journeys at this time, shape-shifting and transmuting. We seek new essences with which to greet the new year.

Now look at your jack-o'-lanterns, dwell on the day, and prepare for a journey to a place deep within yourself.

Long Pause

Close your eyes and take three deep breaths.

Long Pause

You are standing at the top of a hill, facing a dirt path that leads down into a ravine, forested on both sides with maple and alder, fir and cedar. The leaves of the alder and maple have turned to burnished bronze and red. As you begin your descent, a cool wind blows past; a spray of leaves whirl and twist from the trees, filling the air around you. They crunch under your feet and crackle as you follow the path.

Long Pause

The sun is fading, a last glow of orange light peeking over your shoulder from behind you. Twilight falls quickly during this time of year, and night will be here soon. Pick up your pace as you head for the ravine.

Tonight is Samhain Eve. Deep in the forest, the veil awaits . . . the veil that separates the world of mortals from the world of spirits. There are other veils waiting; the doors to all worlds will open tonight, giving you the chance to step through and visit other realms.

The grade of the dirt path becomes steeper, taking you down into the ravine as the cliff sides rise beside you. The path is narrow here, and you can no longer see the last light of the sun. Overhead, the sky turns a dusky violet and will soon fade into velvet indigo. The air chills now, and a gust of wind sends shivers up your spine.

Wind whistles through the trees, shaking the leaves and whispering through the cedar boughs. The roots of these trees grow deep into the earth, holding up the sentinels so they might watch over the land. Here and there, roots break through the path, and you stumble over them in the fading light.

Long Pause

As you enter the forest proper, you notice that the foliage is dense and the path has evened out. Occasionally a rock juts out from the path, and you feel it under the soles of your shoes as you pass by silently, unaware of how long you've been walking. Time has lost any meaning here—pinpoints of distant stars sparkle in the heavens, their light billions of years old as it races through space to shine down on Earth. Continue your journey as the moon rises overhead. Glowing and full, the orb hangs golden and ancient over the land, and your blood rises in response to the sight. Stand for a moment and let the moonbeams fill your soul.

Long Pause

You find yourself picking up the pace as your body seems to skim along the path. A power, ancient beyond time, is calling you, pulling you forward. A rush of wind sweeps past, catching you in its wake.

The wind surrounds you, filling your nostrils with the scent of graveyard dust and moldering leaves, with bonfires and sweet apples and hearth smoke. Breathe deeply; inhale the scent of autumn, the scent of the Wild Ones, as you are caught up in the call of the Hunt, the cry of the Huntress.

Long Pause

Now you race along, tripping over stone and twig. Suddenly the forest opens out, and you stumble into a clearing. The wind dies down, and you see that you have come to the center of a ring of standing stones.

In the center of the ring is a large bonfire, sparks crackling up into the night. The stones are twice the height of a man, thick granite slabs and pillars with ancient runic markings etched into their sides. You run your hand over one of them, and the hairs on your arms and the back of your neck become stiff as needles of energy race through your body.

If you listen to your pulse, you can hear it whispering, "Back, take you back, take you back."

Long Pause

Your pulse becomes a drumbeat. Listen to the drum.

[Note to guide: *The drumbeat should start here. It should not overpower your voice, but should be steady and rhythmic. From now on, maintain a strong rhythm in your words.*]

Listen to the drumbeat.
The drumbeat is your heartbeat.
Listen to the drum.
Listen to your heartbeat.
Breathe in deeply the rhythm of the drums.
Breathe in deeply the rhythm of your soul.
Breathe in deeply the rhythm of your heart.
Listen to the drumbeat.
It flows throughout your blood.
It flows with even rhythm.
Beats an even rhythm.
In this ring of stone, you can feel yourself shifting.
Feel your body melting.
Feel the season turning.
Feel your body changing.
Feel your soul spinning deep into your past.
Deep into yourself.
Deep into your nature.
Listen to the drumbeat.
Listen to the drums.

Long Pause

And now in this ring of stones, the drum begins to move you; the drum begins to call you. The fire glowing brightly, can you feel it calling? Listen to the drums. They will tell you what you must do. They will tell you what you need.

Long Pause

Spinning, dancing wildly, go dance around the fire.
Creeping, sneaking, hunting, go crawling through the forest.

Listening, learning, hearing, go spinning through the sky.
Your body changes now; transmute in shape and form.
Transmute into your totem, into animal or being
that best suits now your nature.
Transmute and shape-shift now,
like our ancestors before us,
like the Witches and the shamans,
and the people of the forest
and the people of the jungle
and the people of the desert.

Long Pause

When your task, your journey ends,
you will regain your sense of self
and become, once again, the self you need to be.
You will keep those things for the new year,
that you go now to learn.
Your eyes may open now,
without breaking trance around you,
or keep them closed if need be.
Listen to the drumbeat.
Listen to the drumbeat.
Go now and do its bidding.

[Note to guide: *Now you will, with simple words like "come" and "follow me," lead everyone to the space you have reserved for the dancing. Turn on the music, or if you have drummers, have them start dance beats now.*]

Dance now; dance the rhythms of your totems. Dance the rhythms of your heart.

[Note to guide: *Dancing should continue until you notice people beginning to tire. Before the energy dissipates too much, have one drummer lead everyone back to the meditation area. Everyone should sit near their pumpkins again.*]

Take three deep breaths. Now close your eyes. Listen to my voice.

Extended Long Pause—about one minute

Now, as I count from twenty to one, you will become awake and alert, and the feeling of balance will stay with you as you go about your daily life.

Twenty . . . nineteen . . . eighteen . . . seventeen . . . you are becoming more alert . . . sixteen . . . fifteen . . . fourteen . . . thirteen . . . the sounds around you are becoming clearer . . . twelve . . . eleven . . . ten . . . nine . . . you are becoming aware of the world around you . . . eight . . . seven . . . six . . . five . . . four . . . you will awake clear and refreshed . . . three . . . two . . . one . . . take three deep breaths, and when you are ready, you may open your eyes.

Suggested Exercises for Samhain Meditation

1. Was the animal you turned into the same one you expected to turn into? If not, why do you think there was a difference?

2. This is a very powerful meditation. Some people find it difficult to let themselves go because they are too self-conscious or are afraid of what they might find. Did you have any qualms like this? If so, do you think you can work through them?

3. When you heard the drumbeat, how did your body respond to it? Music affects our heart rate, our pulse, our emotions, and our moods. Do you think you can use music on a regular basis to aid your magical and metaphysical work?

4. Discuss, as a group, the nature of how your totem animal spirits help you in your daily life; how much do their energies affect your reactions to things? How do both their positive and negative qualities reflect in your own behavior?

Yule

Yule is the second Sabbat in the Wheel of the Year, and it is celebrated on the Winter Solstice. An astronomical celebration, it also symbolizes hope in the middle of winter, which in most northern European countries can be fierce and deadly. It is the celebration that welcomes back the sun, and it is recognized as the time when the Sun King, or the Oak King, is reborn to the Goddess. He journeyed into the Underworld at Samhain, and during Yule, he is reborn as the young Lord, and the eternal cycle of birth and death begins again.

Yule is a time of rejoicing; it is a time to make merry and to revel in the comfort of one's family and friends. During the cold winter months, people need some hope to hang on to, some reason for celebration. On the Winter Solstice, they gather to feast and spread enough joy that the sun will want to return.

We see the Pagan roots of this holiday in Christmas today, and most Pagans celebrate Yule instead of Christmas. The Christmas tree was originally the Yule log, Santa Claus was the Holly King, and the legend of the birth of Jesus originated in the stories of the rebirth of the Sun King. *Deck the Halls* is a Pagan song that has come down through the years fairly intact. There are many correlations, and they are easy to find if you want to study this further.

Guidelines for Use

This meditation is appropriate for use during or as preparation for Yule rituals. I recommend you use it on the night before the Winter Solstice. One way my friends and I have celebrated Yule has been to stay up the whole night and welcome back the sun at the break of dawn. This meditation would be a good way to pass the time during the midnight hours, when you truly wonder whether the sun will return.

PLANTS:	*white carnation, red rose, poinsettia, holly*
INCENSES:	*pine, cedar, cinnamon, spice, spruce*
OILS:	*carnation, cedar, spruce, pine, rose, cinnamon*
CRYSTALS:	*quartz, garnet, blue topaz, pearls*
CANDLES:	*red, green, white, gold, silver*

Yule Meditation

Relax and make yourself comfortable.

Close your eyes and take three deep breaths.

You are standing at a window, staring out into the late afternoon. It is snowing outside, thick, heavy white flakes drifting soundlessly down to carpet the grass. The sky is overcast and shines with that luminous silvery blue that accompanies winter snowstorms. It is cold out, chill and frozen, but the wind is kept at bay by the thick windowpanes and the heavy red velvet curtains that sweep down to the floor.

There is a fire in the hearth, and the flames crackle, popping and hissing as the fragrant apple wood burns. It is a comforting sound and an even more comforting warmth.

Tomorrow morning is the Winter Solstice, Yuletide. You have waited for this holiday since Samhain. The rains of autumn have given way to the icy snows of winter, and it seems like years since the sun has shone. As you think back to the golden days of summer and how wonderful they were, a shiver crosses your back. What if the sun doesn't come back? What if, like your ancestors feared, the Sun King is not reborn and winter continues indefinitely?

Long Pause

A noise at the door startles you. It's a close friend, dressed in warm boots and a heavy padded coat. "Are you ready to get a tree?" your friend asks.

You don't really want to go outside, but your friend encourages you, so put on your coat and your boots and follow your friend into the snow.

Long Pause

The wind is fierce; it whips against your face and numbs your cheeks and nose. The snow swirls around, flakes sweeping in miniature whirlwinds, and the crystals land thickly on your jacket and hat. The snow is getting deeper now; at least eight inches cover the ground.

As you follow behind your friend, the path that has been shoveled through the snow is icy and more than once you almost lose your footing. You have to be careful not to go sliding into the snowbanks on either side of the path.

Your friend leads you into a patch of nearby woods. The trees are beautiful fir, spruce, and cedar. Their needles hang low to the ground, cloaked with clean, fresh snow. They stand like shrouded giants, muffled from the world by their coverings of snow.

Long Pause

The shadows of light shift and play as the afternoon slips away. You worry briefly about being caught out in the cold after dark, but then the vibrant white, the purity of the snow holds you in thrall as winter silently woos you.

"You look down there; I'll look around over here," your friend says. "Whistle if you find the perfect tree." As your friend walks into a thicket of spruce, you hear a sudden snap and turn your attention to the path in front of you. A white fox races by and slips into an underground burrow somewhere beneath a cedar. Pass through the copse, out into a clearing. There, you are brought to a sudden stop.

In the middle of the clearing stands a luminous unicorn, glowing white with a pale blue horn made of an icicle. It turns to look at you with shining silver eyes.

Long Pause

"Welcome to the realm of the Ice Queen," she says. Her voice is that of thin glass shattering, like a hundred chimes playing in the wind. "Welcome this Winter Solstice night. I will be your guide while you are in our realm." She turns and calls over her shoulder, "Climb on my back, and I will take you to the Ice Queen."

You easily fit on the unicorn's back, but you wonder about your friend, back in the woods.

As if sensing your worry, the unicorn says, "Do not fret. Your friend will be all right, and you will return here soon."

You settle in place and notice that the wind and snow no longer numb you. The unicorn and whomever she carries are protected from the storm. She starts off at a quick pace and then begins to run.

Long Pause

As she races along, trees and snow go streaking past. Soon she is running so fast that you can only see a blur on either side, and then, just as suddenly as she started, the unicorn stops.

The first thing you notice is that it's no longer snowing. The night sky glitters with stars, and you are standing in front of a palace carved from crystal and ice. It stretches as far as the eye can see and reaches high into the frigid sky.

Long Pause

"Welcome to the palace of the Ice Queen," says the unicorn. "Here my frozen Lady lives with the Holly King. Enter and pay your respects. I will wait here to take you home when it is time for you to return."

The door to the palace opens as you near it. The walls are glistening sheets of ice that rise hundreds of feet into the air. They remind you of glaciers; indeed, they may well be carved straight from those huge mountains of ice.

You walk across the floor. It, too, is made of ice, and you are surprised at how easily you can walk on it. Twin pillars mark the opening to a huge throne room. When you pass between them, a set of chimes peal out with laughter, reverberating through the great hall.

At the end of the hall stands a throne carved out from the walls, and on the throne sits a woman who is at least twice your height. Her skin is the color of twilight, her features rigid and chiseled. She glistens as if she too has been molded from the frozen waters of the world. Long veins of indigo and violet race through her body, and her dress seems to blend with her skin. She stands and glides forward to greet you.

Long Pause

"Welcome to the realm of the Ice Queen." Her voice rumbles with the creaking of glaciers and breaking ice floes. "Come in and be welcome in my chamber." She motions for you to sit on a bench near her throne. She captures your gaze, her eyes the color of blackest night with twin diamonds glowing within their cores.

"Do you understand the true essence of winter?" she asks. "This season is the time when, in these northern regions, the Earth must rest and replenish herself. The Goddess lies in her childbed, awaiting the birth of he who will grow to be her mate. For without the return of the Sun King, the world would wither and die of frost."

She points to a polished and faceted sapphire on the bench next to you. "Look deep into my crystal," she says, "and see the turning of the Wheel." Look into its depths.

Long Pause

A mist forms in the gem and then clears as you watch the images of which she speaks.

"This is the longest night of the year. In ages past, humankind didn't know about the turning of the planets around the sun. Would the sun continue to dwindle and slip away from them, dooming them to disaster? To encourage the return of the sun, people paid homage and gave reverence. They held feasts to cheer themselves and to offer the Sun King a promise of joy to come, for if he did not return they would die.

Long Pause

"The Sun King—the Oak King—lost his battle at midsummer and journeyed into the Underworld, capitulating to the Holly King who rules over the waning part of the year. They battled their eternal battle and, as every year from the beginning of time, the Sun King laid down his sword in defeat.

"But on this day, the Winter Solstice, the Goddess prepares for his rebirth, for his return from the Underworld, and the Holly King waits for the new battle."

Long Pause

As the Ice Queen speaks, you see, in the depths of the gem, a tall man cloaked in furs and holly, grizzled and ever ancient. He stands waiting, holding a sword in front of him. A wreath of holly with red berries surrounds his brow.

As you watch, the stars glitter behind the Holly King as he waits on a field of snow. In the distance, in her bed of lush needles and soft furs, the Goddess lies with pregnant belly and throws back her head, the pains of birth taking hold of her loins.

Long Pause

The stars begin to fade; morning is coming. The Goddess screams as she pushes the young Lord out of her womb. He slides into the waiting arms of a Priestess, who holds him up to the dawn.

The Holly King, sensing the moment is near, raises his sword, and as he faces the morning, a sliver of light appears in the east and then a single ray, faint and feeble but golden, pierces the sky and hits the Holly King in the heart.

He drops to the ground, dead, and an ancient Crone kneels and gathers his body in her arms, then returns to the Underworld with the dead Lord. The Goddess looks on her son and smiles. The Sun King is reborn. And so the cycle plays out year after year, century after century.

Long Pause

The mists swirl back into the gem, and the Ice Queen leans over you. "Do you understand the nature of winter now? Do you see how, without winter, there could be no spring? Winter is, much like death, a respite, a place of refuge from the burgeoning strength that spring and summer require. A time during which to meditate and dwell on those projects you would like to begin. A time of quietude. And, on this, the Winter Solstice, a time in which to revel and rejoice that the Sun Lord has been reborn."

She points to the crystal. "Think of your own life. Think of those habits, people, and possessions that you must sacrifice in order to grow. What must die within yourself to let new shoots appear? Meditate for a moment, then look into the crystal and you will see your answer."

Think on her words, then look into the crystal.

Extended Long Pause—about two minutes

When the mists have again covered the sapphire, the Ice Queen bids you rise. "You must return," she says. "But I give you a parting gift." She hands you a seedling, a small spruce in a blue bucket. "Take this with you, and after Yuletide is over, plant it in the woods."

She walks you to the door, where the unicorn is waiting. You climb on its back and, after you take one last look at the palace, the unicorn races away like the wind.

Long Pause

She returns you to your earlier spot in the forest. When she comes to a halt, silver hooves glittering against the snow, you see that only a few moments have passed since your departure.

"Put your tree on the ground," she says.

As you do, the tree starts to grow. It swiftly branches out until it is six feet high. The unicorn laughs. "Decorate it with care, for you are its guardian. Plant it wisely and in a spot where it will be safe." And then she turns and, like the wind, is gone.

The tree is beautiful, its branches full and sweeping, its roots thickly entwined in a root ball. Now whistle for your friend.

Long Pause

After a few minutes, your friend comes tromping into view.

"What a wonderful tree! Where did you find it?"

If you like, on the walk home, you can tell your friend of your adventures.

Long Pause

As you make your way back through the forest, the last bit of afternoon light fades and dwindles. The snow is falling quickly now; the flakes are smaller and faster, and you can smell ozone in the air, which tells you the storm will be here for at least a few more hours.

You reach your house just in time. Darkness falls as you pull the tree inside. Take off your coat and hat, then carry the tree into the living room where you first started.

The fire is warm and merry. There is a plate with hot chocolate and cookies sitting on the table, and you know that your family and friends are near.

Set the tree up in the corner and begin to decorate it. Every decoration that you hang on the tree means something; each one is special. Spend a little time decorating the tree now, and do not forget where it came from.

Long Pause

As you hang the last ornament on the tree, your friend says, "I'm going to help make dinner."

Your job is fire tender and, when you are alone in the room, you throw another log onto the flames and go back to the window.

It is dark outside now, but you can still see the faint glimmer of the snow as it glides down to carpet the ground. Think about your visit to the Ice Queen's palace. Even though she promised that the Sun King will be reborn, there is a part of you that wonders whether it will truly happen again this year.

Long Pause

Your family and friends have decided to stay up all night to revel and make merry so the young Lord will want to come back. Somewhere in your heart, you know that when he does return, at the moment of his rebirth, you will also mourn the death of the Holly King, in his beautiful and icy realm.

Now, as I count from twenty to one, you will become awake and alert, and the feeling of balance will stay with you as you go about your daily life.

Twenty . . . nineteen . . . eighteen . . . seventeen . . . you are becoming more alert . . . sixteen . . . fifteen . . . fourteen . . . thirteen . . . the sounds around you are becoming clearer . . . twelve . . . eleven . . . ten . . . nine . . . you are becoming aware of the world around you . . . eight . . . seven . . . six . . . five . . . four . . . you will awake clear and refreshed . . . three . . . two . . . one . . . take three deep breaths, and when you are ready, you may open your eyes.

Suggested Exercises for Yule Meditation

1. Sit up all night to welcome back the sun. During this time play music, drum, tell stories, watch great movies, truly entertain yourself so the Sun King will sense the joy in being alive.

2. Look for correlations between the Roman Saturnalia, the Christian Christmas, the Pagan Yuletide, and other celebrations that take place around this time of year. See if you can trace them back to common denominators.

3. A few weeks before Yule, get together with friends and have everyone bring spare bits of ribbon, evergreen boughs, crystals, and other decorations, and have a wreath- and ornament-making party. Suggested materials include:
   - ❖ cranberries for stringing
   - ❖ gemstone chips
   - ❖ popcorn for stringing
   - ❖ molding clay
   - ❖ old charms and coins
   - ❖ silk flowers
   - ❖ dried fruit slices
   - ❖ ribbons
   - ❖ herbal charms
   - ❖ crystals
   - ❖ evergreen boughs
   - ❖ beads
   - ❖ acorns and nuts
   - ❖ bells

4. With a group of friends, reenact the birth of the Sun King and the death of the Holly King. Create your own Yule ritual around this theme and hold it the eve of Yule—the Winter Solstice.

Imbolc

Imbolc (pronounced Im-bolc), the third Sabbat of the Wheel, is a Celtic festival honoring the Goddess Brighid (pronounced *breed*). Brighid is a Goddess of poetry, fire, smith crafts, and healers. Imbolc is from the Gaelic *immolg*, meaning "in milk," and it refers to the time of year when the ewes and cattle are giving birth, when they are "in milk," feeding their young.

Imbolc is celebrated on February 2 (the Christian counterpart is Candlemas), and during this ritual and attendant celebration, dairy products play a prominent role in the feasting.

Another common feature for many Imbolc ceremonies is Brighid's Bed, a basket lined with satin or lace (preferably red or white) in which a corn dolly is laid to represent the Goddess Brighid. This is considered Brighid's marriage bed (notice the similarity between the pronunciation of Brighid and the word *bride*). The corn dolly should be wearing a wedding dress. Carefully lay her onto a satin or silk cushion in the basket and nestle a phallic-shaped loaf of bread next to her. This represents the coming of the God. Much ceremony can be made out of presenting the loaf to the corn dolly, and it is a beautiful addition to any ritual altar.

This is the time of year to pay attention to creativity, to projects that you have begun, to the healing arts, and to productivity in general.

Guidelines for Use

This meditation is appropriate for use on Imbolc. I recommend dressing in red, black, and white for this meditation, and spending some time after the meditation writing, drawing, or participating in some craft or artwork.

PLANTS: *red and white carnations, red and white roses, baby's breath, fern*
INCENSES: *dragon's blood, carnation, vanilla*
OILS: *carnation, vanilla, vanilla musk*
CRYSTALS: *garnet, clear quartz, pearl*
CANDLES: *red, black, white*

Imbolc Meditation

Relax and make yourself comfortable.

Close your eyes and take three deep breaths.

Several weeks past Midwinter, you are standing outside the door of a small log cabin that is your home. Not far away, in a thick stand of pine and spruce, the sound of birdsong echoes as the birds land in the trees and shake the snow from the branches.

Go around to the back of the cabin, to the small shed in which you keep chickens and sheep. The air is crisp, and you find it necessary to tighten your cloak around your shoulders as you push through the new inches of snow that lightly cover the trail to the shed.

As you approach the shed, you can hear the shuffle of the chickens and the raspy voices of the sheep. Enter the shed and look around.

Long Pause

The lambs are still young, and they suckle against their mothers. Make sure the sheep and chickens have enough food to eat and then leave the shed, firmly latching the door so no predators can get in to harm the animals.

You return to the cabin, where you pick up your knapsack and head to the nearby forest. The path is clearly marked and packed snow has become as hard as ice, but the new snow from last night dusts it and gives you a firm footing.

As you walk along, bundled tightly against the cold, the sun rises higher into the sky. Even with the new snow and the crisp early morning air, the day seems warmer than yesterday. While spring is still a month or so away, you know the harshest part of winter has passed.

When you reach the boundaries of the forest, gaze quietly up at the trees. At night they creak and moan in the wind—you can hear them even from your cabin—but today the breezes are silent, and you are actually beginning to feel a little warm. You open your muffler and let the cool air press against your skin.

Long Pause

The sun climbs higher as you enter the woods.

Here the path is easier to navigate. The snow is not so heavy under the thick cover of tree branches, and you increase your pace, making better time. As you pass through the silent wonderland, you occasionally see a branch move or a bush shake, and you know that not everything is asleep, dormant for the winter.

The forest deepens around you, widening out. You have walked for about an hour when you hear the sounds of laughing up ahead, and as the path bends and you turn a corner, you see a group of people gathered around a large well that stands in a wide clearing.

The people in the meadow are friends of yours, villagers whom you've known since childhood, and you have come to join them in celebrating Imbolc, the festival of Brighid.

Long Pause

The people bid you welcome, and you put your knapsack down and join the others near one of the bonfires that burn brightly throughout the meadow.

At one fire, a pig roasts over a spit. Another fire has died down to embers, and potatoes and turnips roast among the coals.

Almost everyone here is dressed in something red or white. Search in your knapsack for your ritual outfit and go behind a large blanket that hangs from a tree. It's private and you can change clothes there. As you change into your ritual garment, feel your workaday, outer self slip away as you dress yourself for ritual and magic.

Long Pause

When the sun is high overhead and midday has come, the village High Priestess calls everyone to feast. The smell of roasting meat makes your stomach rumble, and you gather gladly with the others at long, makeshift tables. Eat heartily, for the ritual begins at twilight, and afterward you know you have the journey home to make.

The foods on the table are hot and filling: meat and bread, apples, potatoes, and turnips. Great jugs of milk have been specially marked for the feast, and wheels of cheese dot the tables. Fill your plate and think about the fare you're eating. Sturdy and sustaining, it is winter food, food that stores well and silences hunger pangs, for summer's bounty is still a long way off, and even spring vegetables seem a distant dream.

Long Pause

After dinner the adults rest while the children play. The fire tenders maintain the bonfires that melt away the snow underneath and they prepare the ritual fire, stacking willow and hawthorne branches, hazel and rowan and oak. Eventually, the High Priestess walks by and summons everyone to gather near the main ritual area. Search in your knapsack and find the candles you were asked to bring. One is red, one is white, and one is black. You also have your ritual chalice with you.

Long Pause

The ritual area is in a large clearing a little farther along in the woods. The ritual fire, or the need fire, has been laid in the center. Split logs surrounding the ritual area have been cleared of snow, and people take their seats in a semicircle. Find a place to sit and wait until the High Priestess steps forward. A tingle in your belly tells you that the magic is near. The energy is running high today, even though everyone seems calm and relaxed.

"Welcome to Imbolc and welcome to our festival," she says. "May Brighid give blessing to the houses that are here, Brighid the fair and tender, her hue like the cotton grass, rich-tressed Maiden of ringlets gold."

As the ancient words of invocation open the ceremony, you find yourself sliding into a trance. The voice of the Priestess is gentle, floating on the wind, almost inaudible as it drifts into your thoughts and out again.

"We gather to celebrate the Lady Brighid, Brighid the Renowned, Brighid the Fiery Arrow of Power, Goddess of fire and fertility, of healing and cleansing, of poetry and smithery, Goddess of the oracle."

The Priestess turns to light the Imbolc fire, and it crackles, blazing to life. The flames flicker high in the air, showering sparks on the frozen snow below.

She speaks again. "Daughter of Dagda, wife of Bres, mother of Ruadan. Yours were the first cries to be heard in Ireland when your beloved son died in battle. On this day we gather to honor you and renew our pact with fire, which rules healing and creativity and the forge."

As her voice dies away, look into the fire. Amid the crackling flames, you see the image of a woman. It is Brighid, and she rises above the meadow, full-bodied and beautiful.

Long Pause

"Take up the black candle of smithery," she says, and it seems that you alone hear her voice. "Decide now what you would have manifest in your physical world this coming year. Hold the candle and envision what you want to build," she says.

Take your black candle and focus your will into it.

Long Pause

When you have finished, get up and walk to the fire. Cast your black candle into the flames and watch it melt away.

Long Pause

She speaks again. "Now take up your white candle of healing, and decide what you want to heal or cleanse in yourself. Hold the candle and envision what you want to purify," she says.

Take your white candle and focus your will into it.

Long Pause

When you have finished, once again get up and walk to the fire. Cast your white candle into the flames and watch it melt away.

Long Pause

A third time she speaks. "Now take up your red candle of poetry and art, and decide what beauty or art you wish to create during this coming year. Hold the candle and envision what you want to create," she says.

Take your red candle and focus your will into it.

Long Pause

When you have finished, for the third time get up and walk to the fire. Cast your red candle into the flames and watch it melt away.

Long Pause

The image in the fire vanishes, and the High Priestess steps forward. She says, "Now, one by one, follow the path into the crystal grove, where Brighid awaits your coming." She points to a short path in back of the fire.

You are the first to rise, and you walk down the path where the trees are bedecked in red and white ribbons, and as twilight deepens into evening, you enter the crystal grove.

Pine and spruce surround the area. The snow is light here, almost magically absent. In the center of the grove is a sacred font, made entirely of crystal, and more crystals rise out of the water, which shimmers with the sea foam shade of aquamarine.

Behind the font, sitting on a pillow of red satin embroidered with gold, is the Goddess Brighid. She is cloaked in red and gold, and her eyes are like two crimson flames. She watches as you silently approach.

Long Pause

At her left hand sits a platter with hazelnuts on it. At her right hand, a platter of salmon. Three jugs of wine sit near her throne.

She motions for you to sit opposite her. "Welcome to the Crystal Grove," she says. "The night is for scrying, for divination. But first you must understand the difference between wisdom and knowledge. Knowledge gives you an understanding of things. Wisdom guides you in how to apply that understanding for the best outcome with the least harm. Think on this for a moment," she says.

Long Pause

She lifts the platter of salmon and offers it to you. "Eat of the salmon of knowledge," she says, and you take one bite of the sweet flesh. Then she leans forward and offers you an insight about yourself or a problem you've been having that you need to resolve. Listen to her words.

Extended Long Pause—about one minute

The Goddess next offers you the platter of nuts. "Eat of the nuts of wisdom," she says, and you take one of the hazelnuts. The nut is carved with the rune of hazel, of wisdom and creativity, and you eat it. Then Brighid once again leans forward. This time she takes your hand and gives an insight about yourself that you've been overlooking. Listen to her words.

Extended Long Pause—about one minute

After you have eaten, she holds up a ladle. "Will you drink of the wine of health, the wine of passion, or the wine of manifestation?" she asks. Make your choice and hand her your chalice. She fills it with wine from one of three jugs and hands it back to you.

Drink deep in her presence; feel the energy of the wine racing down your throat to mingle in your bloodstream.

Long Pause

Now pay her honor, bid her farewell, and depart the grove.

You return to the ritual area, where you see another person headed in for their meeting with the Goddess. Sit and think for a while on what you have learned.

Extended Long Pause—about two minutes

When everyone has finished their turn with Brighid, the High Priestess raises her arms to the fire and says, "Thank you, Great Goddess, for joining us tonight. Be with us as we go about our days during the coming cycle of growth."

The ritual over, everyone rises to leave.

Go up to the fire. There, the High Priestess offers you a torch lit from the Imbolc fire. Now set out for home, using the torch to guide your way.

The forest is crackling with energy. You feel renewed, ready for the coming season as you walk under the cloudy night. In fact, even though it is cold and snowing lightly, you can sense a shift in the air, and you know that spring is not far away.

Long Pause

Now, as I count from twenty to one, you will become awake and alert, and the feeling of balance will stay with you as you go about your daily life.

Twenty . . . nineteen . . . eighteen . . . seventeen . . . you are becoming more alert . . . sixteen . . . fifteen . . . fourteen . . . thirteen . . . the sounds around you are becoming clearer . . . twelve . . . eleven . . . ten . . . nine . . . you are

becoming aware of the world around you . . . eight . . . seven . . . six . . . five
. . . four . . . you will awake clear and refreshed . . . three . . . two . . . one . . .
take three deep breaths, and when you are ready, you may open your eyes.

Suggested Exercises for Imbolc Meditation

1. After the meditation, perform the candle ritual that was described. Find
   birthday candles in black, red, and white and meditate on one of each
   for the three things in which you would like to effect change in the
   areas of manifestation, healing, and creativity. Then light them from a
   central red or white candle and place them in a clear bowl filled with
   clean salt. Let them burn down all the way. This ritual can be done as
   a group or alone.

2. Write a poem, look at what course of action might make you feel
   better, create something physical like a birdhouse, a sculpture, or a
   sewing project.

3. Read Celtic lore about Brighid and the spheres over which she reigns.

# Ostara

The Fourth Sabbat of the Wheel, Ostara celebrates the Vernal Equinox (Spring Equinox). It is an astronomical celebration, and it emphasizes new growth, the return of life to the world, fertility, and the young.

The Christian celebration of Easter has its roots in Ostara. Eostre is the Saxon Goddess of spring, and to celebrate her festival, eggs were decorated to represent fertility. The hare or rabbit was honored as another representation of both fertility and the Goddess, and the focus laid squarely on children, young animals, and rejuvenation and rebirth. Note the correlations; Easter eggs, the Easter Bunny, resurrection, chicks, and baby animals are all prime focuses around this time of the year.

The land is beginning to wake at this time; farmers plant their crops, and new life abounds everywhere you look. The Goddess has weaned the young Sun Lord from her breast, but he is still too young to survive on his own. He is growing, though, and come Beltane he will be the Young Phallic Lord, old enough to embody sexuality and take his place as her consort.

So we celebrate Ostara with eggs and rabbits, with dairy products and sweet cakes, and with the joys of childhood should contain.

Guidelines for Use

This meditation is appropriate for use during the Vernal Equinox. Since this is one of the two times during the year when day and night are of equal length, it might be interesting to look into the astronomical origins of this festival.

PLANTS: *painted daisy, tulip, daffodil*
INCENSES: *heather, lilac, camphor*
OILS: *new-mown hay, lilac, heather*
CRYSTALS: *clear quartz, rose quartz, amethyst*
CANDLES: *pastel green, pastel yellow, pastel pink, pastel blue, egg shapes*

Ostara Meditation

Relax and make yourself comfortable.

Close your eyes and take three deep breaths.

It is a beautiful spring morning. The air is almost balmy. There is still a bit of a chill against your skin, but you know that warm weather is on its way.

Today is Ostara, the Vernal Equinox.

You are standing outside a white wooden house. The house is bordered with flowers: daffodils, tulips, and the last of the crocus. It isn't quite time for the lilacs to bloom yet, though you can see young buds on the tree.

Look up at the sky overhead. The gleam of the sun against the brilliant blue reminds you of a mirror, polished and the color of robins' eggs. There are no clouds right now, though you know they could bank up at any time. Sudden rainstorms are not uncommon this time of year.

Long Pause

Today you have decided to go on a spring treasure hunt to see what has wakened to life in the past six weeks since Imbolc. You have a basket with you and a walking stick, and since the weather is so changeable at this time of year, you decide to wear a light windbreaker and a pair of rubber boots.

The meadow in back of the house stretches far afield, down to a copse of trees near a silver brook. As you prepare to make your way through the meadow, you notice the sky shimmer, as if gleaming waves are folding in on themselves. The air around you glitters for a moment, and you blink.

Long Pause

When you open your eyes, you are still facing the meadow and the house is still behind you, but now there is a subtle difference. Everything seems more vivid and brilliant than it did a moment ago. Pause briefly to let your eyes adjust to the change.

Long Pause

Now slowly wend your way through the meadow. The grass brushes against your knees. It tickles, and you notice that not all of the dew has evaporated yet. As you meander along, a movement in a thick patch of nearby thistle alerts you. A large rabbit, a brown hare, hops out of the grass and across your path.

It stops to look at you with the most beautiful blue eyes you've ever seen, and for a moment you think it's going to speak, and you wonder whether you've entered Alice in Wonderland's realm, but then the rabbit hops off in a different direction and soon disappears. You can see a pile of droppings where it paused, and something shines among the rabbit pellets.

It is a pearl, a perfect and luminous pearl. Pick it up and polish it carefully on your pants.

Long Pause

The pearl is almost as large as your thumbnail, and it reverberates with a gentle hum. As you listen, a warm drowsy feeling begins to tingle from the bottom of your feet and works its way up, spreading through your body. When the wave reaches the top of your head, it fountains out and showers you with a golden rain of tranquillity.

Pause for a moment and feel the sense of peace cloaking you.

Long Pause

After a moment, put the pearl in your basket, in one of the small sacks that you keep there. Continue along toward the creek.

The shallow brook runs swiftly along, babbling to itself and to anyone who will listen. You are warm from your walk, so put down your basket and sit on the grass next to the shore. Dip your hand in the clear water and bring it up to your lips.

The water's icy, cold and sweet, and you take another drink. A high-pitched laughter echoes from the creek. As you stop to listen, the laughter continues.

Look around to discover its source—a being is rising from the stream. A woman, she is formed from the water itself. Her translucent skin glistens with a shimmer of aquamarine, and she throws her head back and laughs again. You realize immediately that you are facing a naiad, one of the water spirits that inhabit grottoes and small, wild streams.

Long Pause

She cocks her head playfully and points to the other shore where a large bull-frog sits.

"Kiss the frog," she says.

You look at her to see if she's joking, but she shakes her head and once again says, "Kiss the frog." When you ask her why, she merely laughs and sinks back down into the water, rippling away with the current.

Long Pause

The frog is looking at you with a bemused expression and, as you hesitantly stand and pick up your basket, it hops on top of a nearby stone and waits.

Cross the stream, carefully balancing on a thin log that stretches from one side to the other, and kneel down by the frog. It blinks once, and its cheeks puff out as it lets go with a loud croak.

Feeling perhaps a little foolish, perhaps a little nervous, you lean down and lightly kiss the frog's head between its ice-colored eyes.

Long Pause

The frog stares at you for a moment, and then opens its mouth and spits out a small gray stone that lands at your feet. The frog hops off the rock and disappears among the reeds along the shore.

Pick up the stone.

It is heavy in your hand, and a shiver of energy races out of the stone to coil around the base of your spine. It curls around your vertebrae, inching upward one by one. See it loop around and through each chakra, cleansing them with a trail of sparkling light.

Long Pause

As the energy reaches your crown chakra on top of your head, it discharges into the air, carrying away all of the static and stagnant energy from within you. You feel lighter; the trail of light has swept up all the old cobwebs of negativity in your aura and released them.

Long Pause

Put the rock in another small bag in your basket and continue over to the copse of trees. The birch and alder are just beginning to bud; small knots of green cover the branches, distinct against the brilliant white bark of their trunks.

A loud chirping startles you, and as you look up you see a robin sitting on a nest. A young kitten has gotten itself stuck in the tree, and now the bird and the cat are facing off. The nest is not very high, so you set down your basket and climb the tree. The cat, more interested in safely getting back down to the ground than in eating the bird, lets you put her in your pocket.

The robin looks at you warily, but then she moves and you see that she is sitting on a clutch of sky-blue eggs. There is another egg in the basket, however. It is crystal, the color of an azure sea, and the robin uses her beak to push it toward you. Cautiously lift the egg out of the nest and put it in your pocket.

Long Pause

The robin settles back on her nest as you carefully descend from the tree. The kitten seems content to sit in your other pocket; indeed, she's purring, so you leave her there as you take out the egg and look at it.

The egg is made of blue crystal; it looks like it could open—there is a seam running down one side of it—but you can't find the latch. Wrap it up and put it in your basket. With the kitten snoring gently in your pocket, you return to the path and follow it deeper into the forest.

The path leads through the trees, past a wide swath of ferns whose fronds are still curled tightly, before it opens out into a small clearing. In the center of the clearing, on a lush mound of grass, sits a young woman. She has hair the color of spun gold and her skin gleams pale ivory. When she looks at you, her eyes are those of the hare and the frog; they are the color of the robin's egg and the sky, and you realize that you are facing Eostre, the Saxon Goddess of spring.

Long Pause

She is clothed in a shimmering dress of glittering pastel veils. When she stands, her feet barely touch the ground, as if a thin layer of air separates Eostre from the grass. Animals surround her; hares and lapwings, lambs and young calves contentedly chew the grass at her feet. Eostre smiles and bids you welcome.

"It is planting time," she says. "It is time to germinate the seeds for the coming season of growth. Come into my garden and plant what you will."

You walk over to her as she motions you in, and she leads you to the back of the meadow where a large plot of tilled earth sits waiting.

The smell of the soil pulls you down on your knees. It is rich and musty, sour and fertile, and you run your hands deeply through the finely turned dirt. It clumps in your hand, and you bring it to your nose and inhale deeply.

Long Pause

The scent rushes past you like a gust of wind, with the promise of growth and virility just below the surface. Eostre watches you, amused. She kneels down and picks up a handful of the soil.

"This is the secret of life," she whispers. "Without this, there would be no world as we know it. We take from the soil; we go back to the soil. It is part of the ever-turning cycle. Today is the Vernal Equinox, the balance of light and dark. Only when we are balanced and centered can our growth be steady and productive."

She looks into your basket and points at the crystal egg. "Eggs are a symbol of fertility, of rebirth and renewal. Nestle your egg in the warm grass."

Place your egg in a cushion of warm grass. The egg opens on its seam. As you pick it up, you see a seed hidden within and the seed falls into your hand.

Long Pause

"This seed represents a project that is near and dear to you," the young Goddess says. "It is something you would like to see grow and flourish as the world grows and flourishes. Think carefully on what that project might be as you hold the seed in your hand."

Do as she asks. Hold the seed in the palm of your hand while you think about the project that is most important to you right now. See it grow, see it flourish, see yourself accomplishing those tasks that lead to a successful harvest. Take a moment to visualize this.

Extended Long Pause—about one minute

When you have projected your vision into the seed, the Goddess Eostre says, "Now you may plant your seed in my garden where, with proper weeding and watering, it will grow to great heights so your harvest might be a success."

She shows you a corner of the garden. Plant your seed now, and think of what it will take to water and feed it during its fragile germination time. Think of the steps you can take to ensure your seed's health and well-being.

Extended Long Pause—about one minute

After you have planted the seed, Eostre helps you to your feet. "Go now," she says, "but remember the seed you have planted this day. It is up to you to nurture it through its tender youth. The treasures you have found in your basket you may keep, tokens to remind you of what spring represents. Cleansing and peace, innocence and growth."

She points to the kitten. "I will take the young cat, for all young ones come under my watchful eye." Give her the kitten. She takes the mewing infant into her arms, and the kit immediately curls up and falls asleep again. "Peace be with you in the coming season, for with all the activity, you will need a quiet space in which to relax."

She walks you to the edge of the clearing and waves as you enter the forest. With one last look at Eostre and her menagerie, you begin the return journey through the birch and alder trees. Pass back through the ferns, then to the brook, where you may take another drink of water if you like. After you cross on the log, reenter the meadow, and soon you see your little white house up ahead.

As you look down at the basket hanging over your arm, you are surprised to find it filled with daffodils and tulips. The three treasures you found on your journey are nestled among the blossoms.

Now, as I count from twenty to one, you will become awake and alert, and the feeling of balance will stay with you as you go about your daily life.

Twenty . . . nineteen . . . eighteen . . . seventeen . . . you are becoming more alert . . . sixteen . . . fifteen . . . fourteen . . . thirteen . . . the sounds around you are becoming clearer . . . twelve . . . eleven . . . ten . . . nine . . . you are becoming aware of the world around you . . . eight . . . seven . . . six . . . five . . . four . . . you will awake clear and refreshed . . . three . . . two . . . one . . . take three deep breaths, and when you are ready, you may open your eyes.

Suggested Exercises for Ostara Meditation

1. Take a walk and see how many signs of new growth you can find. Write about these in a journal, and visit them over the next few weeks, noticing how quickly change happens.
2. Plant a garden and tend to it regularly.
3. Get a book on the art of *Pysanky* (Ukrainian egg decorating), a *kitska*, and some beeswax and try your hand at this incredibly beautiful craft. If you can't find the time for this, you can use paints to decorate eggs (blow the insides out first) or markers. Or buy wooden eggs from the crafts store and paint them to make permanent decorations for the holiday.
4. Have your group make a Green Man out of grapevines and cedar boughs. Use daffodils for his eyes and set him up to watch over the Equinox, then store him away until Lughnasadh, when you can burn him in the sacred fire. Some friends and I made one that was over seven feet tall, and he was very impressive!
5. If the group chooses, donate a few dollars to buy some pretty rocks or crystals to represent the pearl, the blue egg, and the gray stone for each member of the group. During the meditation, the guide can hand them out at the appropriate times so the participants can focus the energy of the meditation into them. Sometimes the simplest aids are the prettiest; the little oval stones that people put in their fish tanks sparkle nicely. And beautiful pebbles can be found right outside.

# Beltane

The fifth Sabbat of the Wheel is Beltane, celebrated on May 1. Beltane is a festival of sexuality and fertility. The Maypole, central to most Beltane rites, signifies the God's phallus, while the wreath atop the pole signifies the Goddess's vagina. The Maypole is traditionally cut by the men, and the men dig the hole in which it is placed. The women fill the hole with dirt and construct the wreaths for the Maypole and for their own heads. As the ribbons around the Maypole are woven during the dance, the wreath slowly lowers, and so the Divine Marriage is symbolically consummated.

The God is now the Young Phallic Lord. He has become the rutting consort of the Goddess, and on Beltane they mate for the first union of the year. It is at this time that the Goddess becomes pregnant with the new Sun King to whom she will give birth on the Winter Solstice.

Beltane signifies a time of burgeoning growth, passion, and strength for us. It is a time to explore our own sexuality (whatever our orientation may be—heterosexual, homosexual, bisexual, or autosexual), and it is a time to play and revel in the magic as spring turns into summer.

Other traditional activities on Beltane include jumping the bale fire, drinking May wine punch made with sweet woodruff and strawberries, dancing, playing games, making flower wreaths, and doing face painting.

Guidelines for Use

This meditation is appropriate to use on Beltane or Beltane Eve. I suggest taking a long, sensuous bubble bath before the meditation. I also suggest you have a variety of your favorite foods available for after the meditation. You might want to watch the movie *The Wicker Man* during Beltane. (*The Wicker Man* is a wonderful pagan movie, although some Pagans object to the ending, which they consider disturbing.)

PLANTS: *daisy, rose, lilac, fern, violet*
INCENSES: *rose, lilac, vanilla, honeysuckle*
OILS: *rose, lilac, violet, new-mown hay, thyme*
CRYSTALS: *peridot, citrine, amethyst, rose quartz*
CANDLES: *purple, green, gold*

Beltane Meditation

Relax and make yourself comfortable.

Close your eyes and take three deep breaths.

You are standing in a grotto near a beautiful pool of clear water. Trees surround you on three sides—cedars and oaks, fir and birch. Interspersed among the silent giants are lilacs, thick blossoms hanging full and purple off old gnarled trunks. The trees are filled with birds; their incessant chatter keeps you company in the quiet forest.

The day is bright; sunlight glimmers off your hair and reflects from tree to tree. The forest radiates with a golden glow as the rays of light pass through thick undergrowth and turn peridot green.

It is Beltane, and you have come here to bathe. Lift your garments over your head and let them drop to the ground. The air tickles your bare skin, playing over your body like soft, whispery kisses.

Long Pause

When you are naked, slide gently into the silent water.

The bottom of the pond reflects with gems—peridot and citrine, amethyst and sapphire all gleam from the sand beneath your feet. This is the Crystal Grotto, full of magic and passion.

Move your feet along the bottom of the sand. As you stir up the silt, reach down and scoop up a handful of the gems. They shimmer in the sunlight and then, as you watch, they melt and pour back into the pool where they once again form into shining jewels.

The spring season has been hectic; you have worked hard to realize your goals and sometimes the effort has been so intense that it feels like you have strained yourself. There has been little time for play during this growing season, little time to relax, and the tension aches in your shoulders and back.

It is said that if you bathe in the Crystal Grotto on Beltane, it will ease your body and wipe away worry and tension from your mind.

Take a moment to think about the stresses that have built up in your life. Bring them to your conscious thoughts.

Long Pause

Now immerse yourself fully in the water. It is cool against your skin, and as you open your eyes, the water soothes any itching and soreness they might experience, even as it moisturizes the rest of your body.

Feel your worries loosen, they are like old scabs ready to flake away. Rise up out of the pond, letting the water stream off of you as it carries away the dust and strain of the past season.

Long Pause

When your body is clean and your thoughts are clear, step out of the pond and let the sunlight dry your skin.

Long Pause

Your clothes are waiting on the ground. Put them on and pick up the backpack that is sitting under a nearby huckleberry bush. The woods are vibrant, anticipatory. Beltane is here, and you are feeling pulled toward the copse of cedars.

As you walk along, the sun begins to grow warmer. You're sweating, but your body is clean and the sweat feels good. If you like, you may take off your shirt, or stop and change into cooler clothes that are in your backpack.

Long Pause

As you wind along the spacious path that leads through the forest, you begin to get thirsty. There's a canteen in your backpack, filled with clear water. Drink deep. As you are drinking, a low rustle from the foliage startles you. A stag steps out of the undergrowth and stares at you with glowing eyes.

Huge, his rack of antlers stretches over five feet from point to point. The stag throws back his head and emits a low cry. Then the deer jumps and races off into the forest. As he runs, you hear the piercing whistle of pipes from the direction in which he is headed, and the music calls you forward.

You find yourself racing behind the stag, following the call. Running through the foliage, brier and bramble snag your feet and clothing, but you pull free and race on. Your feet have never felt lighter; your heart has never jumped so quickly to any tune before.

Long Pause

Trees and bushes fly by in a blur. The only thing you can keep sight of is the back of the buck. With a fleeting thought, you realize you are keeping pace with the animal. Just when you wonder whether you'll ever be able to stop, the pipes fall silent and you skid to a halt. As you sink to the ground, panting, look around and see where you are.

You have landed in a patch of grass dotted with wildflowers. Daisies and bachelor's buttons dapple the verdant grass. In the center of the meadow, you see the stag. He has stopped before a willow tree, whose leaves drape like vines, shrouding the trunk in a cloud of green.

One long leg extends out from behind the tree. At first you think it might be a giant goat, but then an arm reaches out and curls around one of the branches. Then, before you are ready, out leaps a tall figure. His lower torso is long and ends in two furred, hooved legs. Your eyes travel upward, past the massive phallus, along the muscular chest and well-muscled arms to the hands that clutch a set of argent pipes. And then you know. It is Pan, the Goat God.

Long Pause

He grins beneath his bearded chin, and his eyes glitter with mirth and chaos. They twinkle, blue one moment and then brown the next. His hair, dark as the earth itself, spills over tanned shoulders.

"Well met, mortal," he says.

The stag nuzzles at the God, lowering his head so Pan can scratch at the base of the antlers. Pan eyes you speculatively, then says, "It is Beltane, the day of the Rut. You have unwittingly entered Arcadia. You might as well enjoy yourself." Then he claps his hands, and out from the shadow of the willow tree step three young women.

"Attend to our guest," Pan says.

The nymphs surround you; they are luminous, with almond-shaped eyes and skin that glows even in the daylight. One begins to remove your clothing while another oils your skin with ylang-ylang and jasmine. Her hands are gentle, with the lightest caress. The oil's scent rises to your nose. Intoxicating, the exotic perfumes ride the night sky from half a world away, and you catch a brief glimpse in your mind of blossoms entwining in the night, creeping through lush, opulent foliage. The perfume swirls around you, seducing and teasing, soaking into your skin.

Long Pause

Now the third nymph helps you dress in a filmy, silken robe. It feels like you are wearing nothing at all, and the robe is so sheer that your body is visible through the material.

Pan watches from the tree, still grinning. When you are dressed he says, "Today I mate with the Lady. You will be privileged. Not every mortal gets to watch the Divine Marriage."

As he speaks, there is a soft whisper from the entrance to the meadow. You look as a tall woman enters the lea. Golden haired, she is clothed only in a golden girdle and carries a basket of golden apples. The leaf shadows play against her bare breasts and when she arches her back, Pan sucks in a deep breath. The scent of musk fills the air as his phallus rises, thickly erect. His desire coils around you.

Long Pause

He kneels at the Goddess's feet. "Lady Aphrodite," Pan says, "I am privileged to be your chosen mate this day. This is the season of the Rut, and my desire rises even as I smell your scent, see your beauty, sense your power."

When Aphrodite speaks, her voice shatters the air like crystal wind chimes. She says, "Lord of the Forest, mate with me. Fill me with your sacred seed. Let me worship and revere your phallus, that which fathers the forest."

She falls to her knees and takes Pan's phallus in her hands, then slowly licks it to its full length, her tongue tripping along the throbbing veins.

A low roar starts in the back of Pan's throat, and he pushes Aphrodite back on the grass, then spreads her legs with one knee. His hand slips into the sacred veldt between her knees and she cries out, writhing as he works her into a frenzy of passion.

Pan murmurs, "The body of the Goddess is to the body of the world. From her all things begin, and to her all things return." Then, with a cry of triumph, Pan plunges into Aphrodite, and the world shakes with their passion.

Long Pause

When they have finished, the two Gods look over at you. Both hold out their arms. "You are indeed privileged, mortal. You have witnessed the *Hieros Gamos*, the sacred marriage. Now come, to the one or both of us that you most desire, and take your pleasure."

The nymphs push you forward. Go now, to either Pan or Aphrodite or both, and spend a while in their arms, progressing as it feels safe and appropriate.

Extended Long Pause—about three minutes

When you are finished, Pan and Aphrodite step back to the willow tree. Pan breaks off a branch and fashions it into a simple reed.

"Take this reed and know that when you play on it, the music will summon my attention, and even if I cannot answer, I will know you called."

Take the reed and hold it, knowing it has the power to alert the God.

Long Pause

Aphrodite holds out a golden apple. "Eat one bite of this apple. It will reveal to you the knowledge of your own sexuality. It will guide you in accepting those parts of yourself that may be fearsome or embarrassing. For all acts of love and pleasure are my rituals."

Take the apple and bite into it. The fruit is sweeter than wine, sweeter than honey. As you chew, listen to your heart and what it tells you about your sexual feelings for yourself and for others.

Long Pause

Then Pan turns to the stag. "Lead this mortal out of Arcadia safely," the Goat God says. "Go now, knowing that carnality is a part of life. As our intellects and our emotions need to be used and honed, so our bodies need expression. Beauty is found not only in the body, but in the heart and the passion that guides it. Now climb on the back of the stag, and it will lead you safely to your world."

As you climb on the back of the stag, Pan and Aphrodite raise their hands and wave good-bye.

Long Pause

The stag races out of the meadow, and once again the trees passing by become a blur. Now, as I count from twenty to one, the stag will bring you back to waking consciousness.

Twenty . . . nineteen . . . eighteen . . . seventeen . . . the stag rushes through the woodland . . . sixteen . . . fifteen . . . fourteen . . . thirteen . . . the stag is beginning to slow . . . twelve . . . eleven . . . ten . . . you have passed through the woods and are nearing the Crystal Grotto . . . nine . . . eight . . . seven . . . the stag comes to a halt next to the pond and you slide off its back . . . six . . . five . . . four . . . you will be fully alert and refreshed . . . three . . . two . . . you will be awake and alert . . . one . . . take three deep breaths and when you are ready, you may open your eyes.

Suggested Exercises for Beltane Meditation

1. Gather with friends and erect a Maypole. Dance the pole and, while you are doing so, remember that this signifies the sacred marriage of the God and Goddess.

2. Build a bale fire (have plenty of water on hand for emergencies) and when it has died down, take turns jumping the embers and making wishes as you do so.

3. Make flower crowns and wreaths.

4. Explore your sexuality with a trusted partner or get to know yourself. There are many good books on self-esteem, connection to the body, and sacred sexuality that offer guidance and inspiration, including my books *Crafting the Body Divine* and *Sexual Ecstasy and the Divine*.

5. Learn about the difference between the magical acts of the symbolic Great Rite and the actual Great Rite. Be aware: the symbolic Great Rite can be just as powerful as the actual Great Rite. It can link the two participants unexpectedly. Don't perform either of these rites without careful thought (especially the actual Great Rite), and don't perform either rite with someone you don't know or with whom you aren't fully comfortable.

Litha

The sixth Sabbat of the Wheel is the Summer Solstice, or Litha. It occurs during the latter part of June, and it is the longest day of the year. The Sun King is at his zenith, the Goddess is in full flower, and the northern hemisphere is in the full height of growth. While the harvest is still a ways off, this time of year contains the most potent energy for development.

Litha is traditionally a time for celebrating the faerie folk as well. You might want to go looking for faeries in the woods during the Summer Solstice, especially on Midsummer's Eve. Shakespeare's *A Midsummer Night's Dream* takes place on this day and is a comical example of what can happen then. Be cautious when working with faerie; not all members of the faerie kingdom are friendly. Some are very dark indeed, two examples being the *annis* and the *kelpie*. There are many types of faerie folk from cultures all over the world. Be very respectful if you go hunting them.

As the Oak King (the Sun King) won the battle at Yule, on Litha, the Holly King regains his throne and begins his rule over the waning part of the year. After this day, the sun begins to fade and is sacrificed by the Crone on Lughnasadh, represented by the spirit of the corn or John Barleycorn. Litha is a celebratory festival, rather than a working festival (a festival more focused on celebrating the season than on working magic).

Guidelines for Use

This meditation is appropriately used during the Summer Solstice or on Midsummer's Eve (the night before the Solstice). Try to spend as much time on this day out in the woods, a park, a meadow, near a lake; in other words, get out of the city if you can. If you can't go to any of these places, sitting in a garden or even on the porch steps will suffice.

PLANTS: *rose, nasturtium, thyme, marigold, sunflower*
INCENSES: *violet, chrysanthemum, tangerine, rose*
OILS: *violet, rose, orange, lime, thyme*
CRYSTALS: *citrine, peridot, gold, carnelian, calcite*
CANDLES: *orange, gold, green, yellow*

Pronunciation Guide

These names or words are found in the meditation and can be difficult to pronounce without a guide:

SIDHE: *shee*
BLODEUWEDD: *blod-oo-eeth*
FLIDAIS: *flid-a-is*

Litha Meditation

Relax and make yourself comfortable.

Close your eyes and take three deep breaths.

Tomorrow is the Summer Solstice, the longest day of the year. You have been away on a long journey, and now you realize that you might not be able to reach home in time to celebrate the turning of the Wheel with your family and friends. You still have a long way to travel before you see the familiar sights of your village and the forest that surrounds it.

It is late afternoon, and the sky is a deep, piercing blue. It is so hot that you are sweating, sticky in the summer heat. Wipe your forehead with a handkerchief and look around.

You are standing on a wide plain, next to your horse. In the distance you see the outline of a great forest. You will reach its boundaries in less than an hour, just as early twilight hits. A sense of sorrow and loneliness washes over you, but you quickly shake it off and climb back into the saddle and nudge your horse along.

Long Pause

As you are riding, you think about tomorrow. Litha, as your village calls it, seems a far cry from Midwinter's Day, although you know that they are two sides of a single coin. On the shortest day of the year, the Sun King was reborn and his light struck down the Holly King. But tomorrow the Sun King reaches his zenith and then fades as the Holly King regains his place over the waning part of the year. From now on, the days will shorten little by little until the harvests, and then the cold rains and snows of winter will return.

You ride along in silence until you reach the edge of the forest. Twilight falls gently, and the echoing calls of birds ricochet through the trees as they swiftly fly back to their nests. Though you know it's Midsummer's Eve, the time when the *sídhe*, the faerie folk, rule, and the legends say only fools travel abroad on this night, you want to get home by tomorrow morning so you decide to ride awhile longer.

Long Pause

The moon is up, full and silver, and it is easy to see the path through the shadows of the oaks and rowan trees that make up the copse.

Your horse balks when you urge it into the forest, so you slip off its back and lead it quietly under the canopy of leaves. The night is warm, the air thick, and a sense of anticipation races through the waiting forest as you step under the canopy of trees.

You have traveled for perhaps half an hour when you notice that the hairs on the back of your neck are standing alert. The air crackles; you can almost see the veins of energy as they filter through the forest. Noises in the undergrowth convince you that you are not alone.

Long Pause

As you forge deeper and deeper into the woods, you suddenly notice a glowing green light coming from behind one of the oaks. There is no sense of malice, so you go over to investigate.

The oak must be several hundred years old. Its trunk is gnarled; you'd swear faces are peering out of the bark. Mistletoe has taken hold here and is growing thickly around the tree. The green light shimmers and moves. You can see that it is an orb of light, and it hovers a moment, then sweeps around behind you.

You turn quickly, but the light swoops again, and this time it almost grazes your shoulder. It is a will-o'-the-wisp, and you sense that it is teasing you.

Long Pause

It follows you back to your horse, and the large beast rears up, spooked, and races farther into the forest. Now you must go find your mount. The will-o'-the-wisp flies back to the oak and as you run after your horse, the glowing ball of light ignores you.

The moon is shining brightly. Roots and branches seem to move, and several times you almost trip over an oak root or a rock. The shadows writhe around you, and the forest looms tall; the trees seem to glare at you as you search for your horse.

Long Pause

Up ahead, you hear a whinny. Your horse has caught his reins on a huckleberry bush near a curve in the path. When you move to free him, a sudden crack sounds from just beyond the bend. You leave the horse where he is and slip behind a nearby oak tree. From there you can peer around the curve in the path to see what is making the noise.

In a clearing in the middle of the woods you see a large grassy barrow. It is covered with primroses, violets, and wild thyme and, as you watch, the top of the barrow rises as if on stilts and a haunting melody whispers forth.

Long Pause

The music is calling you forward. You seem to have no control over your feet, and you find yourself propelled toward the barrow. As you near, you can make out figures wandering around under the faerie mound. Some are dancing, others are eating, a few are keeping watch.

You are noticed as you approach, and a tall, lithe man steps up to greet you. His face is solemn, and his eyes twinkle with the experiences of lifetimes. He carries a bow across his back, and a silver dagger hangs from one hip.

"You are a stranger here," he says. He motions to the barrow. "It is unwise for mortals to be abroad on this night, but since you are here and since our music has called you forth, I bid you come in and meet our Queen. She will know what to do with you."

When you try to answer, you find that your mouth will not open. He takes your hand and leads you forward into the barrow.

There are faeries of every shape and size that you might imagine. Short, tall, thin, fat, humanoid, and some who look far from human all gather around you as you enter the barrow.

Long Pause

Your guide motions them back. "This person must see the Queen. She will know what to do with our visitor."

One faerie, a short, stout woman, hurries into another chamber. When she disappears, your guide turns to you and says, "Sit and be welcome until our Queen appears. I would offer you wine and food, but that must wait. There is a chair over there on which you may rest."

He points to a plush velvet chair. It is ragged with age but still soft and comfortable. You sit down as if in a trance, and the faeries return to their music and talk. They seem almost like shadows to you, as if they are not in the same world but only seen through a lens or a special filter covering your eyes.

The music drifts in and around your senses; a thin note played on the violin, a whisper of drums, the trill of a flute from a distant glade all join to swirl around you, and your heart catches in your throat as you suddenly find yourself longing for something that you've never had, never before known.

Long Pause

A sudden hush fills the room as the door leading to another chamber opens. Out steps a woman so beautiful that the sight of her almost breaks your heart. She is tall and willowy, and her hair shimmers from platinum one moment to ebony another. Her eyes flash with violet light. She is cloaked in a gown as green as the forest itself, and it falls around her with a spray of golden sparkles. As she approaches, all the faeries kneel in her wake.

Long Pause

"Welcome, stranger," she says. "I am Queen of Fey, Queen of the Sidhe, and this is my realm. Some have called me Titania, others call me Morgana, still others have called me Blodeuwedd and Flidais. I am all of these and more." She sits down on a chair the guard brings for her. "What leads you into my woods this night, mortal?" Her tone is solemn, and you suddenly realize that you could be in serious trouble.

You answer that you are trying to get home before morning, that your path leads through these woods.

Long Pause

The Faerie Queen nods gravely. "You stumbled on our barrow by accident," she says. "I will not hold you in contempt then; you have not sought to intrude, and I believe you to be of good heart. I will send you on your way, but you must promise to always leave a bowl of milk outside your doorstep on Midsummer's Eve for my people, and you must plant primroses, violets, or thyme outside your home for us to enjoy. We will then recognize you as a friend to the Faerie."

Think about her request, then give her your word.

Long Pause

She stands up and claps her hands. Two short, winged faeries answer her call, carrying a small golden chest. The Faerie Queen opens the chest, and you see it is filled with gems of all shapes, sizes, and colors.

"What is your favorite color?" she asks.

Answer her.

Long Pause

She reaches into the chest and pulls out a thimble-sized gem of the color you specified. It hangs on a long golden chain. She places it around your neck.

"I offer you this gift. Normally when a mortal stumbles into our realm, we offer food and drink, but that would make you tarry far too long among my people. So I give to you this pendant. The gem carries a single spark from my gown. When you look at this crystal in the sunlight or the moonlight, you will feel me near. If you wish to talk to my people, hold the gem up to the light and speak. They will hear you. Is there anything you would like to ask before you leave my kingdom?"

If you wish to speak to the Faerie Queen or to ask her a question, you may do so now and listen for her answer.

Extended Long Pause—about two minutes

The Faerie Queen smiles and motions to the guard who originally brought you to the barrow. "My guard will escort you back to your horse and see you through the woods."

He leads you back through the throng of faeries, to the opening of the barrow. Together, you cross the green to where your horse is waiting. A faerie is feeding and watering it. He helps you back into the saddle, then leads you along the path. The moon is waning and dawn is near. You were in the faerie barrow most of the night.

Long Pause

The guard leads you to the edge of the forest. You see, up ahead, the trees marking the path to your home. Across the plain the sun is beginning to rise.

"You may go alone from here," the guard says. "Remember, on Midsummer's Eve mortals are ill-advised to walk in the forests. But if you must do so, then make your presence known and announce yourself as our friend. My people will hear you."

Then, like a streak of lightning, he is gone.

As you sit atop your horse, the sun begins to rise in the east. The sky is dusty rose, and golden beams dance across its surface, streaking the pale hues with brilliant light. As you watch, the Sun King rises in all his glory. He is at his zenith today and, even amidst the growing heat, you realize that, after today, the year will wane in the eternal cycle that rules the world.

Long Pause

Take a moment to think about all the projects you have started; think about what still needs to be done before harvest. As the sun grows stronger, hold your necklace up to the light and let the beams concentrate in the gem. You can use this energy to infuse your work later on, after the celebrations that await this day.

Long Pause

Now pick up the reins of your horse and head for home.

Now, as I count from twenty to one, you will become awake and alert, and the feeling of balance will stay with you as you go about your daily life.

Twenty . . . nineteen . . . eighteen . . . seventeen . . . you are becoming more alert . . . sixteen . . . fifteen . . . fourteen . . . thirteen . . . the sounds around you are becoming clearer . . . twelve . . . eleven . . . ten . . . nine . . . you are becoming aware of the world around you . . . eight . . . seven . . . six . . . five . . . four . . . you will awake clear and refreshed . . . three . . . two . . . one . . . take three deep breaths, and when you are ready, you may open your eyes.

Suggested Exercises for Litha Meditation

1. Spend some time outside in the park or a garden, trying to commune with the nature spirits and faeries. Look for simple signs that they are there—a bird watching you while you talk, a butterfly settling on your arm.

2. Make an essential oil that will attract faeries. Some suggestions are violet, thyme, new-mown hay, primrose, cowslip, and lilac oils.

3. Think about goals you made at the beginning of the solar year. Since this is the halfway mark, it's a good time to reprioritize and take stock of your progress. What do you have left to do? What have you already completed? Be sure to congratulate yourself on the successes, however small, because it takes a lot of positive reinforcement to achieve major success in life.

4. Plant primroses, violets, or thyme near or in your home to attract faeries. Remember, faeries are not human; they are a different race of beings, and they don't always play by our rules. Modern literature tends to portray them as cute and gentle, but faeries are wild and free. Do not expect them to behave with a warm and fuzzy attitude. This is not to say that they don't have caring feelings or that they don't become attached to people, but they don't conform to our rules of social etiquette. They can be mischievous at times, or dangerous if angered.

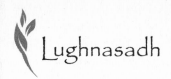

Lughnasadh

The seventh Sabbat of the Wheel is Lughnasadh (pronounced *loo-na-sah*). Lughnasadh is celebrated on August 1, and it honors the Celtic God Lugh, a solar deity. It is also considered the first, or grain, harvest.

This Sabbat celebrates the harvesting of the grain, and it is through this harvest that the God is sacrificed to give life to the people. The God of the harvest is often personified by the spirit of the corn or—as he is better known—John Barleycorn. When the scythe cuts down the grains, it cuts down the God. The Crone wields the scythe, and she is often depicted as Cerridwen, the Celtic Sow Goddess.

During this Sabbat we concentrate on harvesting what we planted during Ostara. We focus on the culmination of projects started earlier in the year.

Guidelines for Use

This meditation is appropriate for use during the harvest festival of Lugh. I recommend a dinner of corn or grain products following the meditation. It is also a good time to review the progress you are making on various projects you currently have going.

PLANTS:	*marigold, corn, wheat, grape, sunflower, ivy, barley*
INCENSES:	*copal, tangerine, musk, patchouli*
OILS:	*musk, patchouli, earth, orange*
CRYSTALS:	*carnelian, tiger's-eye, orange calcite*
CANDLES:	*brown, yellow, orange, corn-shaped*

Lughnasadh Meditation

Relax and make yourself comfortable.

Take three deep breaths and close your eyes.

Our ancestors relied on the harvest to ensure their survival in the coming months of darkness. Today, we rely on supermarkets. But the food still comes from the Earth, and if she falters, so do we. Famine happens; droughts and freezing weather destroy crops. People still starve when the Earth goes fallow. So we turn the Wheel to encourage the weather to hold kind, to witness the sacrifice of the corn spirit so our people might thrive and flourish. On Lughnasadh, the King of the Corn must fall. As the Goddess leads him into her Underworld realm, she begins her own transformation into the Crone of winter's ice and snow.

Long Pause

You are in a protected space, and it is the eve of Lughnasadh, the first harvest, the harvest of the grain and vine.

The evening is warm and twilight approaches. Midsummer's Eve has long passed, and the days are beginning to grow shorter. The sun slips below the horizon a little earlier every night, and there is the slightest tinge of coolness to the breeze. The hint of impending autumn comes creeping in on the early morning air as you wake and crack open the window.

Long Pause

You are standing at the edge of the cornfield, now barren and harvested. The corn dollies have been made for tomorrow, and the last wheat sheaves have been fashioned into guardians against hunger for the coming year. The seed has been saved for next spring's sowing.

There is a tang in the air, a certain crispness that will not fully manifest until the second harvest, the Autumnal Equinox, but the first hints are present in the breeze.

It is a night for vision quest, a night to focus on what you are harvesting into your life and what you are sacrificing. You will choose to let go of some outdated dreams and habits so that other qualities may flourish.

Long Pause

You are carrying a small bag containing all the tools you need this night, so step away from the cornfield onto a path and head toward the woods that lie directly in front of you.

The path is dry from the heat, and your bare feet are warm as they kick up dust. It has not rained for a long time. The silhouette of the forest stands steady against the darkening sky, and as you enter the woods, you can sense the sap running thick in the trees around you. They are already preparing for the long winter's sleep to come.

Small animals rustle in the brush around you, but this night is not for running off to play with the wild, and you leave them to their hunt and continue along the path.

Long Pause

Soon, the path begins to slope gently upward. The grade is still easy, though you are walking at a slower pace, and as the night waxes you find the air a bit chill, so you pull your cloak a little tighter around your shoulders.

Finally, with the moon full over your shoulder, you see what you've been looking for. A path splinters off to your left, marked by a trellis on which grows the sacred vine. Full, ripe grapes, dripping with purple juice, have been left hanging here, for this is the entrance to the Arbor of the Gods.

Long Pause

A sacred well made of agate guards the left side of a pergola. It is dedicated to the Goddess, and you kneel before it in reverence before turning the crank to draw up a bucket of crystalline water.

Use the silver ladle that hangs from the well to dip into the water. Drink and then anoint yourself with the pure, clear liquid.

Long Pause

Now remove your shoes and leave them at the entrance.

You are ready to enter the Arbor of the Gods.

The archway hangs over the path, which is no longer dusty with soil, but now a trail of flat stones set within a grassy bed. They are smooth and do not hurt your feet.

Follow the path as it winds through a wide swath cut through the forest. All around, you can hear the low drone of late-returning bees as they make their way back to the sacred honey hives lining the farthest edges of the path.

The moon is high overhead, past its zenith, and as you look up into the clear sky, an owl glides by, silent in its hunting.

Long Pause

You are nearing your destination—a large circular meadow surrounded by a ring of standing stones. Around the granite monoliths twist thick sturdy grapevines that seem to move as you watch, writhing, showing only hints of the granite below. Most of the grapes have been picked now, but here and there a thick cluster peeks out from below the shiny leaves. In the center of the stone ring rests a wide, flat stone.

Set down your backpack and rest on the cool grass. As you relax, open the satchel and lay out what you've brought.

First, there is a bronze sickle, with a handle carved out of antler.

Short Pause—for a slow count of seven

Next to that you place an ear of corn, still in its husk.

Short Pause

Then a candle and a box of matches.

Short Pause

A small bowl of barley follows, and a scattering of oats.

Short Pause

A bottle of mead rests on the ground now and a piece of felt with cord to bind it.

Short Pause

Lastly, you bring forth a piece of paper and a pencil.

Short Pause

You are set for the night's working.

After you have rested, approach the sacred vines with the sickle. Close your eyes and commune with the spirit of the grape, asking whether you may take a cluster for your rites. When given permission, raise your sickle and cut the vine, removing one cluster, not harming the rest. This will be your food for the night. If you were refused, then you know the God has decided you will not need the extra nourishment.

Long Pause

Next, lay out the felt on the central altar stone and place a pinch of the barley and the oats in its center. You may scatter the rest of the grains around the altar stone in offering.

Now, sit still and let the waning night carry your spirit toward the dawn. As you sit, first think of the harvest and of what you personally want to harvest during this season.

What projects have you started that you want to complete? What tasks have you been putting off that you must catch up with? What personal goals have you shoved aside in the hurry of everyday life?

Extended Long Pause—about one minute

Let the energy of the harvest bring those thoughts to bear. As they become clear, pour the energy into the felt pouch and tie it up tightly, charging the grains within. Know that now you will be able to harvest these dreams and goals and hopes and manifest them into reality.

Long Pause

Lay the pouch on the altar stone and set the candle next to the pouch. Light it with a match from the box and focus on the light, honoring the Sun King who will shortly make his way into the Underworld.

Long Pause

You now notice the first glimmer of dawn on the horizon, above the silhouette of the forest. It is almost morning, and when the Sun King rises, the Goddess will cut him down. He will begin his descent into the Underworld, that the cycle might continue and complete itself. The eternal return, the never-ending Wheel.

It is time to think of sacrifice, of what you are willing and ready to cut from your life, what you need to let go, those things that stop you from harvesting your goals, from being productive and happy, those habits that you continue to do even though they are a detriment. As you stare into the candle's flame, think of what you will sacrifice with the death of the Sun King, the Corn King, that other things may flourish and grow.

Extended Long Pause—about one minute

As the sun rises, pick up the pencil and paper and write down your thoughts. And when you look into the sky, you see now not just the sun, but Lugh the Sun King in the form of John Barleycorn, and Cerridwen, the terrible and wonderful Sow Goddess. She is keeper of the Grail, the sacred drink of wisdom. She is keeper of the cauldron of rebirth, and it is through her that warriors are reborn.

Long Pause

Lugh kneels before her and, with tears in her eyes, she raises a sickle and cuts him down. His blood spills onto the earth in the beams of sunlight, fertilizing and nourishing, preparing the soil for next year's crop. Cerridwen bows her head and turns away, mourning the dead king.

Long Pause

Now take your slip of paper and hold it to the candle where it bursts into flame and burns brightly as a ray of the Sun King's blood illuminates it.

Long Pause

After your rites, take up the corn and look deep into it, for it is the grain of life. What secret does it tell you?

Long Pause

Now, having harvested your crop, having made your sacrifices and looked to the mystery of the corn, open your mead and drink to replenish yourself and eat your grapes to nourish yourself.

When you are finished, gather your tools into your satchel, and with respect, take your leave of the sacred Arbor of the Gods.

Long Pause

You quickly find yourself back on the forested path, and now you see the early morning birds chirping on their branches. The air quickens as the Wheel turns, and you are grateful to know you had a part in it.

Continue down the path, back through the woods, back to the edge of the cornfield. There, your friends and family are preparing for the festivities of the day, and you suddenly feel invigorated, exhilarated, ready to join in, for the grapes and wine have given you new vitality and all weariness slides from you as you race to greet them.

Now, as I count from twenty to one, you will become awake and alert, and the feeling of balance will stay with you as you go about your daily life.

Twenty . . . nineteen . . . eighteen . . . seventeen . . . you are becoming more alert . . . sixteen . . . fifteen . . . fourteen . . . thirteen . . . the sounds around you are becoming clearer . . . twelve . . . eleven . . . ten . . . nine . . . you are becoming aware of the world around you . . . eight . . . seven . . . six . . . five . . . four . . . you will awake clear and refreshed . . . three . . . two . . . one . . . take three deep breaths, and when you are ready, you may open your eyes.

Suggested Exercises for Lughnasadh Meditation

1. Review what progress you have made during the past months. What do you still need to do? How can you alter events so you harvest fully what you desire?

2. Bake bread, and during every part of the process be aware of the energy of the grain, talk to it, feel the yeast as a living entity.

3. Bake cornbread in a man-shaped pan. Decorate it with berries for eyes and ivy vines to represent Lugh, then behead him on Lughnasadh, remaining fully aware of the sacrifice represented. Give the head to the garden and share the body with your friends as a sign of communion with the God.

Mabon

Mabon is the eighth and last Sabbat of the Wheel of the Year. It is considered the second harvest, the harvest of fruits. It is also the celebration of the Autumnal Equinox.

Another astronomical festival, Mabon is generally considered the Pagan Thanksgiving, and it is the time when we gather together to celebrate and rejoice in the abundance of the harvest and the fruits that the Goddess and God have given us. Many Pagans like to contribute to food banks at this time of year, though we should remember that hunger is not limited to the harvest season. Sharing our good fortune with others should be a year-round activity.

It is also a time to remember our ancestors, though, unlike Samhain, this festival is merry rather than solemn, a last big bash before the bad weather sets in. There are many three-to-four-day festivals at this time when Pagans gather to celebrate the season. (The Northwest Fall Equinox Festival is one such gathering, held in Oregon every September during the Equinox. For more information see appendix 2.)

Guidelines for Use

This meditation is appropriate for use on the Autumnal Equinox. Like Ostara, it is a time of balance—day and night being equal. You might want to study the astronomical consequences of this holiday and how they affect our planet.

I suggest using this meditation in a group setting, perhaps after a late-afternoon feast. While dinner is digesting and people are in a quiet, mellow mood is a perfect time to have your guide lead you through this journey.

PLANTS: *gourd, pumpkin, dried sunflower, statice, apple, walnut, almond, hazelnut*

INCENSES: *spice, cinnamon, orange, tangerine*

OILS: *clove, cinnamon, tangerine, orange*

CRYSTALS: *gold, citrine, rose quartz, moonstone*

CANDLES: *orange, brown, tan, yellow, pumpkin-shaped*

Mabon Meditation

Relax and make yourself comfortable.

Close your eyes and take three deep breaths.

Summer is over. The leaves on the trees burn brilliantly; shades of orange, yellow, and bronze emblazon the forest with color. The nights are cooler, and there is a chill in the morning air when you wake.

You are standing at the edge of a vegetable garden. Today is Mabon, the Autumnal Equinox, and the first frost hit the ground last night. The sun is filtering through the trees, but you can still see the delicate lacings of white that glitter across the vines. You know that when the sunlight touches the vegetable garden, the frosted vines will wither and blacken. There is much work to be done today.

Carry a large basket into the tomato patch and begin picking the green tomatoes. As you pick each fruit, wrap it carefully in old newspaper and tuck it gently into your basket. The tomatoes will sit in a dark basement in a single layer where they will ripen slowly without rotting if you do not bruise them.

Long Pause

When you have picked all the tomatoes that are left on the vines, it's time to mulch the plot. You have been raking leaves the past few days, and now you have a huge pile of them that you covered with a light piece of plastic to protect them from the rain. Take large armfuls of the leaves and layer them across the tomato vines. With a garden fork, turn the soil and mulch the leaves under the fresh earth, spading up the plants as you go. The soil smells musty, almost sour, and you know that autumn is here. You have spent several weeks canning the fruits of the garden, and now it is time to put the bed to rest.

Long Pause

After you have finished, take the tomatoes down to the basement. There, on well-ventilated shelves, stand rows of squash and pumpkins, full and orange and waiting for Samhain.

Your pantry gleams with jar after jar of corn and peas and peaches. Bags of dried beans and sunflower seeds sit waiting for inclusion in casseroles and breads. Stand back and look at this bounty with pride. It has taken a lot of work to encourage the growth, but now you have a good stock put away for the winter, and you know hunger is not likely to knock at your door.

Long Pause

This afternoon you will gather with your neighbors for a feast. Everyone is bringing a different dish, and you have agreed to make a hearty soup. Look through the different vegetables and choose several—corn and peas, the rich tomato stock you made earlier this summer, a few potatoes from the burlap bag in the corner, an onion, a large zucchini, and a scoop of dried beans. When your basket is full, leave the basement and climb the stairs that lead to your kitchen.

Long Pause

First you need a big stockpot. It should be sturdy and solid, representing a centered, well-balanced you, and it should be big enough to hold all the ingredients that go into producing a fully balanced and enriching soup.

Now look at each vegetable that you are going to add to the soup. Each vegetable represents a challenge you have met and mastered, a goal that you set and were able to accomplish. As you prepare each vegetable and drop it into the pot, think about your goals this year and the successes you can count for yourself.

Extended Long Pause—about one minute

Are there some vegetables that are missing? Remember that even with all our best intentions, sometimes things don't work out the way we hoped or planned. Sometimes the universe has other ideas about our lives, and sometimes chaos intervenes.

Think now about those goals that you were not able to meet, that still have not come to fruition. Have you allowed them enough time to grow? Does their season take longer than you thought? Do you still need to forge ahead and give your energy to them or should you let them quietly die and put them to rest in order to create new space in your life?

Extended Long Pause—about one minute

When your vegetables are chopped and cleaned and in the pot, add enough vegetable stock to cover them and turn the burner to medium heat.

While the soup cooks, you have time to pay your private reverence to the Goddess. Go back to the basement and get a large pumpkin and a small basket of apples. Then change into a warm ritual robe.

Long Pause

Return to the garden. The work you did this morning looks good, and when you look at the vegetable patch, a sense of pride in your honest labor wells up and fills your heart. Next to the garden patch is a wide, flat stone. On this stone you placed an ear of corn at Lughnasadh; it has now thoroughly dried, and today you add to that the pumpkin and the basket of apples.

Long Pause

Kneel by the stone and touch its smooth surface. The rock is warm to your fingertips, but not with the intense heat of summer, and you know that winter is coming soon.

Look at the food on the altar, then around at the fields standing barren and parched. The body of the Goddess is tired; she must rest. But out of her soil came food for the winter, wonderful fruits and tangy vegetables, grain for the cattle and sheep, berries for the birds and the wild creatures that live in the forest beyond your farm.

This is the cycle, the chain of life. Fruit springs from the earth and is eaten so we may live. But death is an inevitable part of life, and when we die, we feed the earth so life may grow again.

From death to life to death to life again, and on and on. The eternal turning of the Wheel.

Long Pause

Take time now to thank the Goddess for the fruits she has brought into your life, both tangible and intangible. Dwell for a moment on those things for which you are grateful.

Long Pause

Now return to your kitchen.

There is a knock at your door. A steady stream of friends arrive to celebrate the harvest with you. They bring symbols of the abundance that the world has given to them—one a loaf of bread, another a pie, a third grew no food but worked hard to produce a wonderful poem that lifts hearts.

Another friend enters. This one wrote a book that entertains and enlightens her readers. Still another brings a box of dreaming pillows to share with others. He is a craftsman and hand-stitched every seam with love and care.

One friend grows livestock; he provides a turkey, roasted and stuffed with savory dressing. A bowl of corn, a cake, a jug of wine, a bowl of miniature animals carved from cedarwood to be worn as amulets are all placed on the huge table.

Look around at all the people with whom you will share this holiday. Friends and family, even strangers, you have all come together for one central purpose: to honor the abundance in this world and to give thanks for your participation in the great chain of life.

Long Pause

As everyone forms a circle, holding hands, take a few minutes to concentrate on each person that has played an important part in your life. Do you tell them that you are happy to know them? Have you ever given them a little gift "just because"? How often do you let the people you love know that you care about them? Do your friends always have to call you, or do you take the time to reach out to them?

Extended Long Pause—about one minute

Now, as everyone has gathered to feast and make merry, make a pledge to yourself that over the next few weeks you will return any neglected calls, you will write a few letters that you have been putting off, and you will take time to remember the less fortunate in this world.

What can you do to make the world a better place? How can you help the planet rather than harm it? Can you volunteer a few hours per month to teach an illiterate person to read, to help out at a homeless shelter, to visit the sick or the elderly at a hospital?

Long Pause

Think about something that you can do to give back for all the wonderful gifts and services you have received in your life. For only when we share, whether it be a few dollars to aid injured animals or a few hours to feed hungry people, do we truly understand the joy that giving brings.

Now, as I count from twenty to one, you will become awake and alert, and the feeling of balance will stay with you as you go about your daily life.

Twenty . . . nineteen . . . eighteen . . . seventeen . . . you are becoming more alert . . . sixteen . . . fifteen . . . fourteen . . . thirteen . . . the sounds around you are becoming clearer . . . twelve . . . eleven . . . ten . . . nine . . . you are becoming aware of the world around you . . . eight . . . seven . . . six . . . five . . . four . . . you will awake clear and refreshed . . . three . . . two . . . one . . . take three deep breaths, and when you are ready, you may open your eyes.

Suggested Exercises for Mabon Meditation

1. Prepare a harvest dinner to share with friends to welcome the season.
2. Spend Thanksgiving Day helping out at a homeless shelter, serving food to those less fortunate than yourself. Better yet, gather a group of friends together to do this. It can be fun.
3. Create a harvest wreath out of dried corn, nuts, dried oak leaves, acorns, grapevines, and other seasonal bounty.
4. Invite an elderly neighbor over for dinner once a week, or make a casserole for that young single mother down the street, the one who has too little money and too many pressures. Or offer to baby-sit for her one evening a month, or maybe give that elderly neighbor a ride to the pharmacy when she needs it.
5. Organize a food drive.
6. Ask owners of neglected fruit trees if you can harvest the fruit and either use it yourself or distribute it to friends, neighbors, and hungry people.

PART 4

Deities and
Dimensions

Artemis

Artemis is the Greek Goddess of the Moon. She is known as the Virgin Goddess of the Hunt. She represents the wild, free part of woman, untamed by motherhood (although Artemis looks after mothers and their young), unencumbered by the restraints of a committed relationship. She longs to race into the forests, to run off to the big city, to savor and experience life on her own terms without worrying about how it concerns anybody else. She is represented by the bear, the stag, and the dog. Her worshippers include athletes, hunters, dancers, lovers of nature and wild places, Witches, archers, and healers.

While many people associate Artemis with the waxing moon because they see her as a virgin or the Maiden Goddess, I do not limit her to that role here. If she is Goddess of the Moon, then she is Goddess of all its phases. Since legend connects her to the Hunt, which runs under the full moon, I have chosen that phase of the lunar cycle for the background of this meditation.

When we undertake a meditation dedicated to Artemis, we go in search of the wild parts of ourselves that long to run with the hunt, that need to be free from city streets and daily pressures. If you are feeling a need for these things, you may want to take some time to get away, go to a park or go camping. Reconnect with the natural part of yourself that is locked up during days at the office or behind the counter. In other words, *play.*

Guidelines for Use

I created this meditation for use during the full moon. I suggest bathing in water scented with lemon and lavender first, and I also recommend making almond cookies or tea cakes to share afterward or have some acceptable light sweet available.

Be aware that all meditations focusing on specific deities will call in those energies, so pay respect where it is due and understand that, while some Gods and Goddesses have a sense of humor, not all do (see Pele). Don't automatically assume that you can make jokes at their expense. I have found Artemis to be an intense Goddess, passionate about her realm. While she seems to care about humankind, I make sure to honor her every time I invoke her, whether it be through a meditation or ritual.

PLANTS:	*rose, jasmine, honeysuckle, fern*
INCENSES:	*patchouli, jasmine, rose, cypress, cedar*
OILS:	*cypress, pine, olive, rose, jasmine*
CRYSTALS:	*moonstone, clear quartz, amethyst*
CANDLES:	*white, silver, green*

Pronunciation Guide

SIDHE: *shee*

Artemis Meditation

Relax and make yourself comfortable.

Close your eyes and take three deep breaths.

You have entered sacred space, where time and trouble have no bearing, where the mundane is swept aside to make way for the art of magical callings and clear sight. The moon has reached her zenith once again. She is full in the night and glowing silver. Let me take you on a journey to her realm.

The day has been filled with trouble, stress, and the everyday pangs of living. You have been on errands to the village today, and as you head for home, all you can think of is bed and sleep.

Long Pause

The path home leads near the sea, and you strike out as twilight descends, hoping you can make it before dark. There are many side paths in this land; you haven't explored most of them, and it would be easy to get lost. Keep your eyes on the trail, not looking toward the sea or the sky, and slowly begin the ascent toward your village.

You walk for what must be thirty minutes, growing sleepier with each step, and finally you realize you must have taken the wrong path. Too tired to continue or to retrace your steps, pull your cloak tight around your shoulders and lie down in the soft grass to sleep.

Long Pause

When you wake, it feels like hours have passed. Get to your feet. You find that you climbed up to a cliff top, far above the crashing sea below. A few more steps and you would have fallen over the side. The waves are strangely quiet tonight, silently rolling up to kiss the shore.

The moon is full overhead, gleaming silver in the night. By the moonlight, you can see that the cliff on which you stand is barren and craggy, with wild, pointed rocks jutting to the sky. As you peer over the side, you can see the water, sea foam glistening in the moonlight.

A cry rings out behind you, and you look around to see what is there. As you walk to the other side of the path, you see forest below, with a narrow trail leading down into the lush woodland. The cry comes from somewhere in the forest.

Stretch out, reach for the sky to loosen your muscles. Sleep has left you somewhat refreshed, and you realize that it's useless to look for the path home right now. It's too dark to recognize any of the landmarks, and it would be foolish to rely on luck.

Long Pause

As you stand there, trying to decide what to do, once again a cry comes racing up from below. It sounds like a woman screaming in the night, not a scream of fear or anguish, but a scream of power, like that of a great cat who prowls the jungle. Your blood races to the call, and your limbs begin to tingle.

As the call fades away, another rises to take its place, this time the howl of wolves, and a pulse begins to ripple through the ground, rising up from the woodland copse. It's the pulse of a drumbeat, starting slowly, then rising in tempo and volume, and as it beats, you find it hard to remember where you are or what your name is.

Long Pause

The beat is hypnotic, powerful and strong.

The wolves howl again, and this time you understand their cries. "Come join us," they beckon, "come join our Hunt."

You look up into the sky, where, against the full and silver moon, the silhouette of a woman rises. Strong and muscled, she carries a bow in her hand, and over her shoulder hangs a quiver of arrows. A silver crescent with a large, glowing moonstone gleams on her brow, and around her neck a string of quartz beads holds a bear pendant carved from pearl.

Long Pause

Standing in a swirl of jasmine and ginger, when she sees you watching, she throws back her head and laughs. Your feet suddenly itch to run. You feel strong and captured by the moonlight, which shines in your eyes and reflects on your hands.

Then, with a rush, Artemis goes racing by, leaping off the moon to lead her Hunt. Behind her race two wolves and then a bear, and you find yourself swept up in the current, and you are running, chasing with the Hunt as it heads into the forest below.

The forest seems to glisten and sparkle, and you barely feel the path beneath your feet. You are going so fast that you can't even tell whether you are breathing, but it doesn't matter because you are in the realm of the Gods, and the wind sweeping back from Artemis's wake will sustain you.

Long Pause

Fir and cedar and oak and thorn go by in a blur of glowing light, as various animals of the forest join the Hunt. Squirrels and deer, stags and snakes, a hawk joins in, and then a panther. The line of animals grows as you run, inexhaustible and full of life. A group of centaurs join the race; half man, half horse, they gallop along behind you on the cushion of air that keeps you all aloft.

Long Pause

Then come the Sídhe, the faerie, winged sylphs, and glowing green flame dancers; gnomes rise from the earth to fall in the Moon Goddess's wake, and undines climb from their streams to flow along beside you.

You race with the Hunt, through the night, watching the moon climb into the sky. It is difficult to gauge how many miles you've run; the forest seems to go on forever. Just when your body shows signs of weakening, when you sense faint hints of weariness, the Hunt begins to slow. You are walking, suddenly alone in the deep forested night.

Long Pause

Still in reverie, enchanted and filled with the lingering beat of the drum that now rests in silence, you see a glowing light ahead. You follow the path, and it leads to a clearing. As you step into the clearing, you see all the animals of the Hunt milling about. The faerie and centaurs are in their midst. In the center of the clearing sits a great throne carved of ancient oak, and in the center of the throne sits Artemis. Two wolves guard one side of the throne, her bear the other.

Long Pause

She beckons you forward, and as you step closer you see that a birch stump stands before the throne, luminous in the moonlight, and on the stump rests a silver bowl surrounded by white ginger flowers. The silver bowl is filled with clear water, and moonlight reflects against the rippling surface.

"Look into the water," she says.

When you look into the bowl, the water shimmers and shifts.

Long Pause

"I give you a gift," Artemis continues. "Hear my spell as you watch the water.

"In the water you will see

A glimpse of what you need to know,

As I will, so mote it be,

Now look into my silver bowl."

Again, look into the water and see what gift of sight Artemis has given to you.

Extended Long Pause—about one minute

When the vision begins to fade, the water shifts again, and you see a crystal palace in its moonlit reflection. Among the crystal shards rest silver orbs, shining against the quartz.

Artemis says, "Make a wish based on the vision I have given you. Then reach into the water and take one of the silver tokens."

Do as she asks.

Long Pause

When you have the silver token in hand, Artemis says, "Keep this gift in a sacred space as a reminder of our visit. If you wish, on the next full moon, toss it into the ocean waters, and it will carry your energy out to the waves and return it multifold. Remember, it has been blessed by the Goddess of the Moon. You have run with my Hunt, you have answered my call; do not forget that we have met. Remember me. In the light of the moon, see me."

You find yourself growing sleepy. You curl on the soft ground by the feet of the Goddess, safe and protected, and sink into a deep sleep.

Long Pause

When you wake it is morning, and you are lying in the grass near the path that leads you home. The sun is shining, and you open your hand and see the silver token of Artemis resting snugly there.

As you stand up, your body is free of all tension, and you shake your head to clear the cobwebs then make your way home.

Long Pause

Now, as I count from twenty to one, you will become awake and alert, and the feeling of balance will stay with you as you go about your daily life.

Twenty . . . nineteen . . . eighteen . . . seventeen . . . you are becoming more alert . . . sixteen . . . fifteen . . . fourteen . . . thirteen . . . the sounds around you are becoming clearer . . . twelve . . . eleven . . . ten . . . nine . . . you are becoming aware of the world around you . . . eight . . . seven . . . six . . . five . . . four . . . you will awake clear and refreshed . . . three . . . two . . . one . . . take three deep breaths, and when you are ready, you may open your eyes.

Suggested Exercises for Artemis Meditation

1. Create a scrying bowl like the one in the meditation. Take a silver or crystal bowl and place a cluster of quartz crystals in the center. Fill it with Full Moon Water (see appendix 2), and then drop dimes or silver charms in the water. Use this to scry with.

2. Go camping for a weekend and spend your time watching and observing the wild fauna of the area.

3. Take archery lessons. The sport develops the eye and coordination. When you are practicing, think of Artemis.

4. Spend one warm summer month charting the phases of the moon. Stay up all night on the waxing, full, waning, and new moon nights and meditate on the differences in energy.

Pele

When my husband's stepmother sent us airplane tickets to Hawai'i so I could meet his family, I looked forward to the trip as I had none other. His family lives on the Big Island, where Pele, the Hawaiian Goddess of volcanoes and fire, makes her home amid the lush, tropical vegetation.

Pele is real. Of all the Goddesses I've worked with, Pele has made herself the most known and felt in this—the human—world. The Hawaiian people are an extraordinarily spiritual people. Their culture is a living, breathing entity. When you get away from the tourist spots, the Hawaiian lands and life are among the most beautiful I have encountered. The land is vibrant, hormonally young and active. Lava fields stretch for miles, destruction beyond anything I could imagine and yet, within that destruction is the creation of new land—the youngest land on Earth.

In the center of that creation and destruction stands Pele. Pele-honua-mea, Woman of the Sacred Land. Pele-ai-honua, Eater of the Land. Tutu Pele, Grandmother Pele. She is serious and caring. She is jealous and vengeful. She is sensuous and volatile. But most of all, she is there.

Pele lives in Halema'uma'u Crater, along Crater Rim Drive in the Hawai'i Volcanoes National Park. Halema'uma'u is one of many craters that make up the Kilauea Volcano.

Pele is not confined to her crater. Hawai'i is her land. She created it with her molten rock, and one can feel her presence everywhere. She cares for her children; she takes care of those who respect her, but if you overstep your boundaries, Pele will eat you up.

If you ever visit Hawai'i, be aware that to remove rocks from Hawai'i is like stealing a part of Pele's body. It is an act of disrespect, an act of theft, and many people have felt Pele's wrath until they mailed or took the rocks back to Hawai'i. Do not take this curse lightly, it is very real.

The *Pele Meditation* is intended to give you a feeling of the Goddess and her beautiful land. There are many places I could not touch upon in such a brief experience, but this should give you some flavor of what it's like to stand on the doorstep of a Goddess.

Guidelines for Use

The *Pele Meditation* was written to give you an idea of what I call tropical fire: the merging of lush passion, incredible fecundity, and the stern, barren wastes created by the lava. In a land of extremes, Pele is the center point.

PLANTS:	*white ginger, plumeria, orchid, hibiscus*
INCENSES:	*white ginger, jasmine, hibiscus*
OILS:	*ginger, ylang-ylang, narcissus, jasmine*
CRYSTALS:	*obsidian, clear quartz, coral*
CANDLES:	*red, orange, green, yellow*

Pronunciation Guide

Many of the Hawaiian words used in this meditation are much easier to pronounce than they look.

A'A:	*ah-ah*
HALEMA'UMA'U:	*ha-lay-ma-oo-ma-oo*
HAWAI'I:	*ha-vhae-ee*
HILO:	*hee-lo*

HINA:	*hee-na*
HUALALAI:	*hoo-ah-la-la-ee*
KILAUEA:	*kee-la-way-ah*
KOHALA:	*ko-ha-lah*
MAUI:	*m-ow-ee*
MAUNA KEA:	*m-ow-na kay-ah*
MAUNA LOA:	*m-ow-na lo-ah*
NA-MAKA-O-KAHAI'I:	*na-ma-ka-oh-ka-ha-ee-ee*
O'HELO:	*oh-hay-lo*
ÒHI'A LEHUA:	*oh-hee-a lay-hoo-ah*
PAHOEHOE:	*pa-ho-ee-ho-ee*
PELE:	*peh-leh*
PELE-AI-HONUA:	*peh-leh-ah-ee-ho-noo-ah*
PELE-HONUA-MEA:	*peh-leh-ho-noo-ah-may-ah*
PUNA:	*poo-nah*
TUTU PELE:	*too-too peh-leh*
WAILUKU:	*wa-ee-loo-koo*

Pele Meditation

Relax and make yourself comfortable.

Close your eyes and take three deep breaths.

You have come to the Big Island, the Island of Hawai'i, because it has called to you. For a long time you put off your visit and then, one day, you could wait no longer but made the long journey here to find out who or what has summoned you.

It is early morning. When you woke, the hillsides were covered in mist. The sun is slowly burning away the clouds, and the day promises to be lovely. The humidity is high, but the temperature is not as hot as you expected it to be.

Today you are going to visit the Kilauea Crater. Everyone here seems to just say, "We're going to Volcano." There are several volcanoes on the Big Island—the peaks of Mauna Loa, still active, Hualalai, a dormant volcano, and Mauna Kea and Kohala, both presumed extinct. But you are going to visit Kilauea.

When you mention that you are going to visit the volcano, people tell you, "Take breath mints. You'll need them at the Sulfur Banks."

The drive up to the park begins in Hilo. The town is lovely, small enough to be friendly, yet spread out along the southern Hilo coast. Before you leave Hilo, you stop by Rainbow Falls. Situated on the Wailuku River, you find Rainbow Falls along the western outskirts of town.

Nestled in a lush grotto filled with ferns and palm trees, with brilliant red heliconia, lush anthuriums, and plants that make your philodendrons at home look like dwarves, the waterfall is guarded by a sturdy rail lining the cliff side. From here, you can watch the Wailuku River tumble over the edge with a thundering roar as it crashes down to the riverbed below.

Long Pause

Behind the waterfall, you can see a cavern, so wide it is almost rectangular. Someone sees you looking at it and says, "That's where the Goddess Hina lives. There was once a dragon who tried to kill Hina. He lived at Boiling Pots, farther up the Wailuku. Hina's son Maui begged Pele to give him some of her molten rocks. She acceded, and Maui threw them into the river at Boiling Pots where the dragon lived and scalded it to death, so Hina was free from the dragon's attacks."

If you look into the foaming spray of the waterfall, you might be able to make out the vision of the lovely Hina.

Long Pause

The journey to the volcano takes you south. As you leave southern Hilo you enter Puna, the district most sacred to Pele. You wonder, as you drive through the verdant foliage, what all the talk of devastation is about. From here you can see no scorched land. Indeed, the air is filled with the intoxicating scent of tropical flowers, swirling through you like heady wine.

Long Pause

The grade slowly steepens. The foliage thickens with banana palms and litchi trees. Wild orchids fill the undergrowth entangled with the jade vine flowers.

The air begins to cool a little. You start to see 'ohia lehua trees, the blossoms sacred to Pele. You know that to pick them is to incur her wrath. Along the road you also see the sacred ohelo berries. If these are picked, some must always be offered to Pele before you can safely eat them.

Long Pause

You are driving through what appears to be a natural tunnel formed by filmy trees that shiver in the wind; they stretch across the road to entwine with one another. Then, before you know it, the road opens up and ahead you see a dark building with a sign reading Kilauea Visitor Center.

Get out of the car and look around. You still don't see a volcano. There is no real evidence that you are on a dangerously active geological hot spot. But a friendly ranger hands you a map and suggests you drive around Crater Rim Drive and down the Chain of Craters Road.

Long Pause

Your first stop is the Sulfur Banks. Now the foliage has thinned out. The plants seem drier, except for the occasional copse of fern. You are standing in what looks like a giant quarry, except that instead of gravel it is filled with chunks of steaming yellow sulfur. The smell gets in your mouth, tasting like rotten eggs, and you remember the breath mints in your pocket. They help dilute the taste of the sulfur but even so you are careful not to breathe too deeply here.

Long Pause

You follow Crater Rim Drive until you come to the Steam Vents. Here is your first real view of the immensity of Pele's home. Only a thin wire-and-wood fence separates you from what used to be a vast lake of molten lava. Now hardened and stretching farther than you can see, the darkened surface of the crater still steams here and there. There is no break on the horizon, only rifts and terraces left by the repeated rising and falling of the lava lake interrupt the barren wastes.

Long Pause

The hardened lava runs from shades of tan to brown to rust, depending on what flow it was from, and as you stand there the wind whistles by, stunting the sparse growth that dared take hold along the cliff sides. You notice movement down in the crater and, to your surprise, you see people wandering across the hardened surface. The crater is so vast that they seem miniscule, and you can't help but think that at one time the crater was filled with molten rock and that deep underneath the surface, magma still churns and boils.

When you finally turn away, you hear a faint call on the wind, but there is no one there.

Long Pause

Your next stop takes you to Pele's home, Halema'uma'u Crater. Here, Kilauea still steams and churns; Pele is awake and active. Ropes barricade all but a small walk out to the crater's edge. The smell of sulfur is thick in the air and signs warn of the dangers of volcanic fumes.

Long Pause

You summon your courage, knowing that even though the Hawaiian volcanoes are considered gentle in the world of volcanology, this is still a very dangerous place to be. Here nature shows her untamed wildness; here nature shows no mercy for human folly.

The boardwalk leads to a shrine overlooking the crater. Here people leave offerings to Pele, perhaps some fruit or money, a bottle of gin, a flower lei. Think for a moment about what you would like to leave to honor the Goddess and then place it carefully on the shrine.

Extended Long Pause—about one minute

Halemaʻumaʻu is deeply furrowed with terraces where the lava lake rose and hardened, then fell and hardened. Steam rises from the surface, and rocky chunks of lava dot the surrounding rim. As you stand there watching, you suddenly see a vision. It is a woman, tall with hair the color of spun caramel. Her eyes glow red with fire, and she wears a red dress with white flowers on it. By her side stands a little white dog, and you know that this woman is Pele.

Long Pause

She gazes down at you and says, "What would you ask, to know me and my land?"

If you have a question, you may ask it now and listen for her answer. If not, then simply pay your respects.

Extended Long Pause—about one minute

After visiting Halemaʻumaʻu Crater, you begin your journey down the Chain of Craters Road. Mile after mile of devastation greets you, great swaths of blackened lava, the swirling pahoehoe that pillows up in waves and the chunks of aʻa, razor-sharp edges jutting out of the abstract blocks. Here and there you see lava trees, sculptures formed where the lava engulfed a tree and hardened around it as the wood burned. Sparse, dry vegetation dots the landscape; scrub brush takes hold even in the most barren places.

Long Pause

For twenty miles you drive through the wastes. The road dips down and, as you curve around a bend, you see in the distance a wide expanse of blue; you are heading toward the ocean. You see hanging over the water what appears to be a thick white mist, but as you fully turn the bend you see now that it is steam, rising from the shore.

Your descent levels out next to the shore, and you realize that you are nearing the place where Pele creates new land, where she is fighting with her sister Na-maka-o-kahai'i, the Goddess of the waters.

Long Pause

You pull to a stop and a ranger waves you out of your car. From here you will have to walk. The road leads along the coast, but when you have walked for only five minutes, you find the pavement blocked. A lava flow overcame the asphalt, cutting off traffic. The hardened pahoehoe glitters under the sunlight, pillows stretching with wide fingers to cover the road and land, going out to the very edge of the shore and falling off into the sea.

Long Pause

Ropes barricade your way. Foolish tourists have ignored the warnings and lost their lives when they broke through the crust into hot lava. The magma still flows under the blackened exterior, and you can hear the hiss and pop from here; the steam rises as Pele intrudes on her sister's domain, widening the island, creating new land.

Long Pause

Where the steam billows into the air you can see cinders pop up; black chunks of rock explode as the lava hits the water. If it was nightfall, you would see the red glow of the molten rock lining the coast, but for now the cinders and clouds of steam tell the story of the forces of creation.

As you sit on the hard pahoehoe covering the road, the eternal struggle between fire and water permeates the very air around you. It is wearying beyond description, and you suddenly feel tired and sleepy. The world never rests, never stops moving and evolving.

Long Pause

Watch the steam for a while longer and then decide that you have seen enough for one day. Get in your car and begin the long drive back up Chain of Craters Road.

Long Pause

As you reach the Kilauea Visitor Center once more, you feel a sudden weight lift from your shoulders. The vegetation seems wonderful to you, a relief from the mile after mile of devastation through which you have just passed.

Night is coming. There is little twilight in Hawai'i, just a sudden darkness as the day disappears.

On your drive back to Hilo, you see a woman flagging you down. She asks for a ride into town and, feeling no menace, you let her climb in. She is wearing a dark, long dress, and her face is difficult to see in the dim light. She sits in the backseat and asks for a cigarette.

Long Pause

You look in the glove compartment and find an open pack sitting there. She takes one and thanks you. You are tired from the day, too tired to speak, and your passenger is equally silent. When you see the lights of Hilo up ahead, you turn to ask her where she's going, but the back seat is empty.

The cigarette, half-smoked and stubbed out, is sitting on the seat. There is a sudden burst of laughter around you, and you realize that you have just met Pele-honua-mea in one of her few joking moods. The cigarette butt is a souvenir so you won't forget your visit.

Now, as I count from twenty to one, you will become awake and alert, and the feeling of balance will stay with you as you go about your daily life.

Twenty . . . nineteen . . . eighteen . . . seventeen . . . you are becoming more alert . . . sixteen . . . fifteen . . . fourteen . . . thirteen . . . the sounds around you are becoming clearer . . . twelve . . . eleven . . . ten . . . nine . . . you are becoming aware of the world around you . . . eight . . . seven . . . six . . . five

. . . four . . . you will awake clear and refreshed . . . three . . . two . . . one . . . take three deep breaths, and when you are ready, you may open your eyes.

Suggested Exercises for Pele Meditation

1. Rent a *National Geographic* video on Hawaiian volcanoes.
2. Pursue a geological exploration; are there any volcanoes in your area? Washington State has many (Mount Saint Helens is among the most famous since its eruptions in 1980). How do the volcanoes on the mainland differ from those in Hawai'i?
3. Obtain a piece of obsidian, volcanic glass, and see whether you can feel any energy coming from it.
4. The Hawaiian religion and Hawaiian spirituality differ in many ways from northern European Paganism. Scott Cunningham's book *Hawaiian Religion and Magic* is a good place to start your study if you are interested in learning more.

Taliesin

Minstrels and storytellers through the ages have remembered the story of Taliesin, the first Bard. The Celtic tale goes thus:

Cerridwen, Grain and Sow Goddess, was mother to the world's most beautiful girl and the world's ugliest boy. She decided to create a drink for her son that would give to him all wisdom and knowledge and balance out his deformities.

She was brewing this drink in her cauldron when she was suddenly called away. Before she left, Cerridwen summoned her servant, Gwion Bach, and instructed him to stir the brew, but under no circumstances was he allowed to taste it.

Gwion did as he was told, but some of the grall, as it was called, splattered onto his fingers. Without thinking, he licked three drops of the drink off his fingers and was imbued with the knowledge meant for Cerridwen's son. Cerridwen immediately knew what happened and, in a rage, went after Gwion.

Gwion changed into a salmon, and Cerridwen changed into a pike. Gwion changed into a sparrow, and Cerridwen changed into a hawk. Finally, after a number of shape-shiftings, Gwion changed into a kernel of corn. Cerridwen turned into a hen and ate him up.

When she changed back into herself, the Goddess was pregnant. She gave birth to Taliesin, who was Gwion transformed after partaking of the grall. Taliesin became the first Bard of Wales. He rules over shape-shifting, writing, poetry, music, wisdom, knowledge, and magic.

The meditation dedicated to Taliesin explores the ability to shift consciousness, to touch aspects of life outside ourselves, and to find a safe space for creativity within our own minds.

It is when we can envision and transform our perceptions that we are able to understand experiences beyond our own and so infuse our creations with universal symbols with which others can identify.

Guidelines for Use

This meditation can be used whenever you are feeling a need to expand your powers of creativity. It is useful when you are experiencing a block or plateau.

I recommend using the *Listening to the Breath Exercise* first. It will help clear your mind in preparation for the *Taliesin Meditation*.

This meditation requires a form of relaxation known as progressive relaxation. You should adapt it to your own physical capabilities. Wear loose, comfortable clothing and have a pillow or comfortable cushion on which you can rest.

PLANTS:	*sage, lilac, white carnation, laurel leaf*
INCENSES:	*cedar, honeysuckle, pine, frankincense*
OILS:	*cedar, lemon, lavender, camphor*
CRYSTALS:	*clear quartz, lapis lazuli, clear calcite*
CANDLES:	*white, yellow, lavender, blue*

Taliesin Meditation

Relax and make yourself comfortable.

Close your eyes and take three deep breaths.

Pay attention to your toes and feet. I want you to tense them, and hold for a count of one . . . two . . . three . . . four. Now gently stretch them, letting the tension flow out through the soles of your feet and relax.

Long Pause

Bring your attention up to your ankles and calves. Once again, tense them and hold. One . . . two . . . three . . . four. Now stretch and relax and feel any stress flow out of your legs.

Long Pause

Next you come to your thighs and buttocks. Tense the muscles and hold for a count of one . . . two . . . three . . . four. Stretch and gently release. Let all of the tension drain away.

Long Pause

Suck in your stomach, tense your abdomen and chest. Hold for a count of one . . . two . . . three . . . four. Stretch and relax, let your breath come freely and without strain.

Long Pause

Now tense your shoulders and arms . . . one . . . two . . . three . . . four. Shake them gently and release.

Long Pause

Tighten your scalp and facial muscles. Hold for one . . . two . . . three . . . four. Relax, stretch, and yawn.

Long Pause

All tension floods out of your body, leaving you at peace. Now, readjust your position, making sure you are comfortable, and take three long, deep breaths, exhaling slowly and evenly.

Long Pause

You are sinking deeper and deeper into an altered state of consciousness. Follow my voice.

I want you to reach out with your mind. It is late evening, and you find yourself floating above your house. The night is calm; the winds are still. A lone crow flies by, and you watch as it lands in a nearby tree.

Look up into the sky. The stars are reeling overhead; there are so many that you know you could never count them all. The moon has risen low over the horizon. It is a waxing moon, and the silver crescent gleams against the dark sky.

Long Pause

Float higher, see the roof of your house grow smaller and smaller. You drift past telephone poles and street lamps. Eventually you pass the tops of the very tallest trees and are still rising in the sky.

Your ascent is effortless; it is easy and safe, and you feel no threat or menace as you drift higher and higher into the night.

Long Pause

Now you can barely see the ground below. The lights of the city twinkle almost like stars themselves, but you can't make out the individual houses. As you rise higher, your ascent quickens and you find yourself not just floating now, but actively flying. Spread your arms out and feel the rush of air pass by as you speed higher and higher.

Take another deep breath and let it out slowly.

Long Pause

You are passing through the clouds now. Great wisps stretch out across the horizon, and static electricity crackles across the clouds as you pass up and through the mass of vapor.

Take another deep breath; again exhale slowly and evenly.

Long Pause

You are beyond the clouds, and your ascent quickens even more. You can no longer see the ground, but rise faster and faster until you are speeding along like a rocket.

Suddenly you find yourself orbiting the Earth. Watch as it rotates, a great blue marble in the sky. Now fly up and out of orbit until you are floating in the middle of a vast field of stars.

Long Pause

Everywhere you look, great stars hang heavy in the sky, which extends to all sides. There is no up or down here, and you cannot fall even though you are floating in the middle of the universe.

Now focus on your body. See yourself as you are. Out here you are not bound by the physical laws of the Earth. You find yourself shape-shifting. There is nothing to prevent you from changing your form.

Take three rhythmic deep breaths and let them out slowly.

Long Pause

Feel your body shifting as you change into a cat standing in a patch of tall grass.

What kind of cat are you? What color? How does it feel to have four legs instead of two? How does it feel to be covered with fur? Try to talk and feel your words come out in meows.

Now focus on your whiskers; they act as radar. Try to sense the world around you through your whiskers. Take a moment to experience being a cat.

Long Pause

Now take another breath and shift back into yourself.

Long Pause

Once again, breathe and shift.

This time you find yourself turning into a salmon, a sleek, muscled fish splashing upstream through a river. You make no noise; you have no extraneous limbs. How does it feel to be one long, sinuous body? What does the water feel like against your scales?

Struggle forward against the current. Fully immerse yourself in your fishness.

Long Pause

Take a slow breath and return to being human.

Long Pause

Once again your body shifts, and this time you become a hawk, soaring through the sky. Your wings glide effortlessly on the wind currents. You are hunting, searching for prey below. Feel the drafts of air catch you up under your wings. See with your piercing eyes; search the ground below for your meal.

You spot a mouse running across the field and suddenly you drop, racing toward the Earth at a dizzying speed. For a moment it seems as though you will dive straight into the ground, but at the last moment you pull up, the mouse in your talons, and again you ascend into the sky to fly away.

Long Pause

Change back into yourself. Breath deep, once . . . twice.

Long Pause

Now you are changing shape again. This time you become a tree, rooted deep in the ground. What kind of tree are you? Are you coniferous or deciduous? Are you from Europe, or the tropics, or the Americas?

Feel your roots as tendrils snake down through the ground. This is how you feed, how you drink. Focus on the sap rising through your body, then feel the season change. Is your consciousness slowing down? The sap runs slower, your leaves change color, fade, and die. Your needles stop growing.

How do you experience life as a tree? Take a moment to immerse yourself in this shape.

Long Pause

Now return to your original shape. Reorient yourself in being you.

Long Pause

Now, once again, let yourself shift. This time you will alter your gender. If you are male, you find yourself growing breasts. Your penis recedes; instead, you have a vagina. Feel your hips widen and your muscles become more compact.

Long Pause

You might find you feel more vulnerable. Women have more reason to be fearful in this world. You are not taken as seriously as when you were male. You have a 25 percent chance of being raped. You walk down the street amidst catcalls. If you are fat, you are considered unattractive. If you are beautiful, you are often considered cold and manipulative.

Long Pause

If you are successful in your chosen profession, you often have to soothe the jealous egos of men who are not used to women making more money or having more prestige than them. At home, you might have to do all the housework as well as your chosen career because your husband does not want to help you.

As a woman, you most likely can have children. How does it feel to know that you can bear life inside you. Is it frightening? Exhilarating?

Long Pause

How does it feel to know that your sex included such women as Marie Curie? Emily Dickinson? Queen Victoria? Charlotte Brontë? Katharine Hepburn? Sappho?

Your sexual heritage includes such Goddesses as Gaia, Demeter, Cerridwen, Kali, Hecate, Artemis, and Aphrodite. Their powers are your lineage as a woman. How does that make you feel?

Long Pause

If you are female, you find your breasts shrinking. Where your clitoris was, you are growing a penis and testes. Your strength increases and your muscles grow.

Long Pause

Know that as a man chances are you will die sooner than you would have when you were female. You have more power in the world; your words are taken more seriously. Know also that you can be sent away to fight in wars, to die for causes you might not believe in.

You are often expected to compete for money and power even if it is not your natural inclination. If you cry in front of most of your friends, you will be considered weak and unmanly. You are expected to be polygamous by nature and if you are not, you are laughed at.

Long Pause

You walk down the street and you know that women are afraid you might want to hurt them. How does it feel to know that they don't want you walking near them because they're afraid to trust you?

You can no longer bear children inside your own body, but your seed fathers those children. How does it feel to be distanced from the birthing process by gender?

Long Pause

How does it feel to know that your sex includes such people as Robert Frost? Plato? Socrates? Galileo? Walt Whitman? Sean Connery?

Your sexual heritage includes Gods such as Odin, Pan, Ptah, Lugh, Frey, Hades, Neptune, and Dagda. Their powers are your lineage as a man. How does that make you feel?

Long Pause

Now slowly shift back into your regular form. Become yourself once again. What did you learn from this experience? Do you have more compassion for the opposite sex? Did you find common experiences that make us all human? What did you discover about yourself from this shape-shifting? Take a moment to search your thoughts.

Long Pause

Now look at the universe in which you are floating. Across the field of stars stretches a vast gold-and-silver web. You are seeing the web that connects everything that exists in all times, all spaces, and all dimensions.

Reach out and grab hold of a single strand. Feel it reverberate in your hand, ringing with energy. It pulses and surges with knowledge and power.

Long Pause

Whenever you need to, you can touch this universal consciousness. It will connect you to all wisdom and power, and you do not need a spirit guide or guru or even a God to put you in touch with it. The energy is yours to use anytime you want. You just need to understand that, through your own connection, you can reach others.

Long Pause

This universal connection brings with it responsibility—even as we have the ability to affect others, we must do so with caution and care. No one is totally independent; your actions affect your friends, strangers, and the planet itself.

Now, see a door hanging in front of you in the middle of the stars. When you open this door, it will lead you into a room of your own choosing. You can furnish it however you wish. You can have musical instruments in the corners, great works of art hanging on the walls. The masterpieces of literature can fill the shelves.

If you want a window looking out onto a wide meadow, the window will be there. Whatever you need to inspire your creativity and replenish this part of your soul will be found in this room.

Open the door. Take a few minutes to explore and furnish your room.

Extended Long Pause—about two minutes

When you have filled the room with whatever you need, sit down in the most comfortable spot. Close your eyes and let yourself relax.

If your creativity has been blocked, I want you to now visualize the problem. If you do not know exactly what it is, see the problem as a nebulous gray cloud.

When you can see the problem, ask yourself what you need to do to get rid of it. Sometimes just letting it work itself out will be the answer. Sometimes you need more time to think, or to play. If you can't relax, it will interfere with your creativity.

Long Pause

If you can't hear an answer, don't worry. Your subconscious mind is now actively probing the question. Often the solution will make itself known when you are dreaming or thinking about something else.

Now look around the room again. This is a safe space for you to retreat to when you need some quiet time. All you have to do from now on is get comfortable, relax, and close your eyes. Then say, "I want to be in my Creativity Room," and you'll find yourself here.

Now it is time to leave and return to Earth. Close the door behind you; the room will be safe until you come again.

Once more find yourself floating in the universe.

Long Pause

Visualize the planet Earth. You are suddenly speeding toward the planet. As I count from twenty to one, you will return to this world, return to your body, and wake to full consciousness.

Twenty . . . nineteen . . . you see the planet up ahead . . . eighteen . . . seventeen . . . you are in orbit around Earth . . . sixteen . . . fifteen . . . fourteen . . . you are flying down into the atmosphere . . . thirteen . . . twelve . . . down past clouds and birds . . . eleven . . . down, slowing down . . . ten . . . you see the ground below you now . . . nine . . . you see the lights of your town . . . eight . . . you are now flying among the treetops, and you are heading toward the roof of your house . . . seven . . . you are entering your house . . . six . . . you are returning to your body, settling in gently . . . five . . . you will be fully awake and aware . . . four . . . three . . . your eyes are beginning to flutter . . . two . . . you will be fully relaxed and alert . . . one. Take three deep breaths, and when you are ready, you may open your eyes.

[Note: I suggest you eat something very substantial after this meditation to ground yourself in the physical world once more.]

Suggested Exercises for Taliesin Meditation

1. After this meditation, if you are in a group, take turns discussing the shape-shifting and what you learned, especially about the opposite sex. Creative artists, especially writers, must strive to understand the opposite gender.

2. Every day for the next two weeks spend half an hour focused on a creative project. Accept no interruptions and do not feel guilty about

the time you set aside for this. Artists in our society are not highly encouraged, and we are often made to feel like our art is a luxury rather than a necessity.

3. Research one of your favorite authors or artists. Read about this artist's life and work habits. Get to know the artist as a person as well as a creator.

4. Look at your environment. Is there a way you can make it more conducive to your creativity? Redecorate, change the furniture around— find a way to shake up the static that has accumulated in your physical life.

# Underworld

The Underworld is the realm where our subconscious self exists. It is the realm of death, of hidden truths, of the parts of our psyche that we often are unaware of. Be aware, I am not talking about some version of Heaven or Hell, although most mythologies contain their own likenesses of these two extremes. What I am talking about is a place of shadow and silence, where spirits can roam if they choose, if they've been trapped by their own unawareness or some violence that has shell-shocked them as they passed through the veil, or if they've not yet reincarnated. These astral realms are places where our own living souls can journey for brief times to discover knowledge about ourselves and our lives, either through astral projection or symbolic journeys (guided meditations).

During the symbolic journey into (and out of) the Underworld we make a pilgrimage to the core of our souls, to transform ourselves. We see this mirrored in the legends of the Sumerian Queen of Heaven, the goddess Inanna, when she descended into the Underworld, stripped bare, naked as she stood before the very essence of death embodied by her sister, Erishkigal. Erishkigal was, in essence, the shadow side of Inanna, the Crone where Inanna was the Mother.

If we examine the nature of death at its core, we find pure transformation. When we journey into the Underworld while still alive, we do so in the footsteps of Inanna as we choose to face our shadow-selves and to shed light on all of our aspects, both positive and negative. For to be strong and capable, to eliminate the fear of what we *might* do or be, we must examine both the light and shadow sides of our psyches and accept both as necessary for balance and wholeness.

When we return from our Underworld journey, we return transformed, having faced our deepest fears, having faced the truth of who and what we are. We are better for accepting and acknowledging our shadow-selves.

To understand life, we must understand death. Death is the ultimate physical transformation, and when we go through cycles of change in our daily lives, we are undergoing forms of death in life.

There are numerous Gods and Goddesses who rule over these realms, including Kali, Erishkigal, Anubis, Apep, Hel, Persephone, Hades, Cerridwen, Pluto, Tuonetar, and Tuoni. There are also many paths leading to the Underworld: over the river Styx in Charon's boat, through the forests of shadow in Tuonela, and along the Native American Blue Road of Spirit.

Another way that you can tap into this transformative, introspective realm is through a guided meditation.

During this meditation, I will not be introducing you to any of the Gods or Goddesses listed above. They are powerful and can be very fierce. Instead, you will journey through your personal Underworld with the help of guardian animals.

Guidelines for Use

This meditation is appropriate for use during times of stagnation, when you feel that transformation is needed to advance and grow in your life. I do not recommend using it too often; we must fully pass through each cycle of our life before we can effectively go on to something new.

Perhaps it would be helpful to use this meditation each year before your birthday, a perfect time to assess your growth and plan out your next steps on the road of life.

PLANTS: *lily, white carnation, white rose*
INCENSES: *kyphi, copal, cedar*
OILS: *oakmoss, cypress, cedar, earth*
CRYSTALS: *lapis lazuli, bloodstone, jasper*
CANDLES: *white, black*

Underworld Meditation

Sit back and relax.

Close your eyes and take three deep breaths.

You are standing at the entrance to a cavern. It is evening; the twilight is turning to indigo, and the air is a little chilly. You pull your cloak tightly around your shoulders.

The cavern is rumored to be filled with treasures, not gold and silver or gems and jewels in huge trunks or ancient priceless coins, but the treasure of self-discovery. The rumors say the way is steep and dangerous, and you must wear very stout boots.

It will be dark walking, for the treasure is said to be very far underground, and you will need a light, a lantern. You also decide to take an animal guide with you.

Think of what animal you would like to have at your side. It should be one you are comfortable with, and it can be any size and color you like. Take a moment to think about this, then call and your animal guide will appear.

Long Pause

When your guide appears, ask for its name. Now you must decide what tools you will need. Do you want a walking stick, or do you feel that you need a weapon to protect yourself? Think about it for a moment and whatever you need will appear at your feet.

Long Pause

Now pick up your gear and take a step into the cave. Your animal guide will go with you.

The cavern starts out fairly large and level. It is not easy to see, even with your lantern, and when you look around, shadows seem to loom over you.

When you get to the back of the cave there is an opening just big enough for you and your animal guide to slip through. As you slide between the granite walls, you can smell moss where it is growing on the north side of the cavern.

You are in a long, narrow passage. The floor of the tunnel slopes downward, a gentle grade at first. The passage is only about four feet wide and eight feet high, and if your animal guide is too big to fit in here, you find that it can magically shrink, adapting to the cavern's size.

Long Pause

Hold up your lantern and begin your descent into the tunnel. At first your footing is secure, the terrain is fairly smooth, and you find it easy going, but as you continue along, all the time descending, the slope begins to steepen.

Now and then a rock juts out of the ground; some are sharp and jagged, some smooth. In one place, you find a boulder blocking the passage that is so large that you and your animal guide have to crawl over the top.

Long Pause

The temperature is dropping. It is cold in this granite world, and you shiver as a gust of wind from somewhere far below blows against your skin. It douses the fire in your lantern, and instantly darkness shrouds you in a velvet cloud.

Stop and try to rekindle the light. While you search for your matches, you accidentally drop the lantern, and you can hear it crash, rolling down the slope in front of you.

Long Pause

Your animal guide says, "Stand still for a moment to let your eyes adjust. Then use your other senses to guide you." As you obey, listen carefully to see whether you can hear any noises around you.

Long Pause

After a few minutes, you can make out dim shapes in the darkness, and your animal guide urges you to continue on. If you have a walking stick, it can help you pick out your way. Or you can stretch your arms out and use the sides of the tunnel for balance. You might want to hold onto your animal guide as you walk.

The slope beneath your feet has become quite steep, and you have to move very carefully in the dark to avoid falling. Rocks clutter the passageway; you could easily turn an ankle if you are not careful. Feel each step before you take it; use your internal sense of guidance to keep yourself from tripping over the loose stones.

Long Pause

Now the walls of the cavern feel moist, and you can smell a dank, mildew odor permeating the air. If you touch the granite, you can feel mold growing in slick patches on the stone's surface. Once you think you feel a centipede or some such insect scuttle away from your questing fingers.

Long Pause

Your animal guide encourages you forward. You take another few steps. It is very steep and feels very dangerous, and then your foot touches level stone.

You have come to the end of the passage. Stop for a moment to relax and take a few deep breaths.

Long Pause

You think you hear water in the distance, the sound of a rushing river. You can smell it in the air; the moisture hangs heavy around you. With the help of your animal guide, continue through the tunnel until you feel the edges of the passage as it opens into what seems to be a large cavern.

When you cautiously pass through, testing each step before you put full weight on your foot, you suddenly see a blaze of sparkling light. The walls are covered with a strange phosphorescence. It glitters blue and green and yellow, lighting the cavern with a shimmering glow.

Long Pause

The cavern stretches farther than you can see. There appears to be another entrance on the other side directly opposite you. In the center of the cave, an underground river has broken through the floor, filling a large crater with water to form a small lake. The water smells fresh, but it shines with such an obsidian light that you aren't even sure whether it's real.

Your animal guide leads you over to the edge. "Do not be afraid," it says. "Do not touch the water, but instead look deep into its surface and pay attention to what you see."

When you lean over the edge and look into the dark shining water, you suddenly see an image of yourself. You are lying in a coffin, dead. Your closest friend is talking about you, delivering a eulogy written of truths about your life and your nature. Listen to what is being said. Listen honestly to the truth that is waiting in your soul.

Extended Long Pause—about one minute

Now the pool shifts and changes, and you see another image shimmer into view. This is an image of who you might become. It is not necessarily the ideal you, for there is no perfection in actual life, but an image of how you might realistically, honestly evolve and grow over the next year. Watch and listen to learn what changes you could create for yourself this coming year.

Long Pause

Once again the pool ripples, only this time your animal guide says, "Ask to see what changes you must make in order to bring the last image into reality."

Lean close to the pool and ask, then listen, watch, and learn.

Extended Long Pause—about one minute

Now your animal guide tells you, "This is the river that flows deep into the Underworld. If you have old hurts and old grievances that you are ready to let go, that you have mourned and are now ready to put to rest, then bring them to the surface of your mind and dip your hand into the water. Lift it to your mouth and drink, and those memories will fade into the background of your mind and lose their power to hurt and taunt you."

Think carefully about this. If you are not ready to let go of an anguish, nothing in the world will pry it away from you. But if you are truly ready to go on, to move into the next phase of your life, then drink from the river and let bygones be bygones.

Long Pause

When you have finished, your animal guide says, "The exit on the other side of the cavern will lead you out from this place. Remember, you can never go back the same way you came, not from the Underworld. You will never remain the same after a journey to your inner soul. Stagnation has no power here; change is stability, and transformation remains the goal in this place."

The passage on the other side of the cavern is actually a set of steps carved out of the stone. Your animal guide will remain by the lake until your next call for its help. The steps number twenty in all.

Now, as I count from twenty to one, you will become awake and alert, and the feeling of balance will stay with you as you go about your daily life.

Twenty . . . nineteen . . . eighteen . . . seventeen . . . you are becoming more alert . . . sixteen . . . fifteen . . . fourteen . . . thirteen . . . the sounds around you are becoming clearer . . . twelve . . . eleven . . . ten . . . nine . . . you are becoming aware of the world around you . . . eight . . . seven . . . six . . . five . . . four . . . you will awake clear and refreshed . . . three . . . two . . . one . . . take three deep breaths, and when you are ready, you may open your eyes.

Suggested Exercises for Underworld Meditation

1. Each year, on the day before your birthday, assess your goals to determine whether or not they are still applicable, how far you still have to go to achieve them, and what steps you can take during the coming year to see fruition.

2. Study the varying legends of the Underworld. Find the universal correlations and the differences. Each mythology has its own cosmos and its own Underworld. Make a chart showing the correspondences.

3. Transformation does not usually happen overnight. It is often a slow, tedious process. Look for small successes within the larger goals and celebrate each one as important. True change is a series of steps, not the end in itself.

Appendix One— Correspondence Tables

Yule and Imbolc Correspondences

Direction:	north
Season:	winter
Element:	Earth
Time:	midnight
Colors:	brown, green, white, tan
Guardian Spirits:	wolves, bears, stags, eagles, ravens
Faerie:	gnomes
Incenses:	patchouli, kyphi, frankincense, cedar, sage
Oils:	patchouli, earth, pine, spruce, cedar
Plants:	carnations, amaryllis, poinsettia, mistletoe
Trees:	fir, spruce, pine, holly, birch
Gods:	Dagda, Pan, Cernunnos, Osiris, Herne, Jupiter, Tapio
Goddesses:	Demeter, Ceres, Cerridwen, Frigg, Cybele, Brighid, Mielikki

Ostara and Beltane Correspondences

Direction:	east
Season:	spring
Element:	Air
Time:	dawn
Colors:	white, yellow, lavender, pink, green
Guardian Spirits:	hawk, eagle, wren, robin, peacock
Faerie:	sylphs
Incenses:	honeysuckle, lavender, jasmine
Oils:	honeysuckle, lavender, new-mown hay, lilac
Flowers:	daffodils, iris, tulips, lilacs, crocus
Trees:	alder, apple, cherry
Gods:	Green Man, Ptah, Horus, Frey
Goddesses:	Eostre, Artemis, Kuan-yin, Tara

Litha and Lughnasadh Correspondences

Direction:	south
Season:	summer
Element:	Fire
Time:	noon
Colors:	red, orange, yellow, gold
Guardian Spirits:	phoenix, lizard, dragon, parrot, cardinal
Faerie:	salamander
Incenses:	cinnamon, copal, tangerine, myrrh
Oils:	lime, orange, citronella, musk, ylang-ylang
Flowers:	roses, nasturtiums, marigolds, sunflowers
Trees:	oak, maple, peach, palm
Gods:	Lugh, Balder, Apollo, Ra
Goddesses:	Brighid, Freya, Oya, Pele

Mabon and Samhain Correspondences

Direction:	west
Season:	autumn
Element:	Water
Time:	twilight
Colors:	blue, gray, violet, indigo, white, aquamarine
Guardian Spirits:	shark, salmon, whale, dolphin, goose, heron
Faerie:	undines, sirens, naiads
Incenses:	jasmine, camphor, sage, rosemary
Oils:	lemon, rose geranium, jasmine
Flowers:	dried statice, bouquets of dried leaves
Trees:	rowan, willow, hazel
Gods:	Neptune, Poseidon, Ahto, Manannan
Goddesses:	Ran, Aphrodite, Tiamat, Vellamo

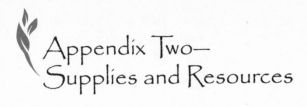

Appendix Two—
Supplies and Resources

Full Moon Water

Fill a clear glass jar with fresh water. Drop a piece of moonstone into the water and cap the jar. During the three nights of the full moon (the night before, the night of, and the night after), place the jar outside where it can collect the energy from the moonlight. This can be used in magical workings that need the energy of the full moon. Each month, add to the water and again set the jar under the full moon.

New Moon Water

Fill a clear glass jar with fresh water. Drop a piece of black onyx or obsidian into the water (be careful—obsidian splinters easily) and cap the jar. During the three nights of the new moon (the night before, the night of, and the night after), place the jar outside where it can collect the energy from the moonshadow. This can be used in magical workings that need the energy of the new moon. Each month, add to the water and again set the jar under the new moon.

Northwest Fall Equinox Festival (NWFEF)

This three-day festival during the fall equinox is held in Oregon. It is sponsored by the Nine Houses of Gaia. For more information write to: Nine Houses of Gaia, P.O. Box 66932, Portland, OR 97290. It would be nice if you included a stamped self-addressed envelope and maybe a dollar or two to help them defray costs.

Resources Guide

Most, if not all, of the shops listed here offer mail-order service and catalogs. Be aware, however, that both retail and online shops go in and out of business with alarming frequency, so some of those listed may not be in service when you write to them, and others will have sprung up since this book was written.

As far as local suppliers go, candles can be found in many drugstores, stationery stores, and gift shops. Flowers can be found at grocery stores and florists' shops. Oils are sometimes found in gift shops, perfume shops, and so on. Crystals can be found in many gift shops or rock shops. Herbs can be gathered wild, purchased through grocery stores if necessary, or found at many food co-ops.

Lovely and unusual altar pieces (like chalices and candleholders) can often be found at local import stores. Altar cloths are easy: go to your favorite fabric store and buy a piece of fabric large enough to cover your altar table.

Finally, don't overlook the phone book. My city has a number of shops listed under various headings, including Metaphysical, Herbs, Books (which often carry far more than just books), Lapidary Supplies, and Jewelry Shops. Sacred Traditions, the local Witchcraft/Pagan shop in my city (owned by good friends of mine who don't do mail order) is listed under "Metaphysical." Small businesses need our support, so don't overlook shops in your own town. They may be hiding under obscure titles!

Magical Supplies

Azure Green
48-WEB
Middlefield, MA 01243-0048
(413) 623-2155
www.azuregreen.com

White Light Pentacles
P.O. Box 8163
Salem, MA 01971-8163
(978) 745-8668 or (978) 741-2355
www.whitelightpentacles.com

Serpentine Music Productions
P.O. Box 2564
Sebastopol, CA 95473
(707) 823-7425
www.serpentinemusic.com

Gypsy Heaven
115G South Main Street
New Hope, PA 18938
(215) 862-5251
www.gypsyheaven.com

MoonScents
P.O. Box 1109
North Conway, NH 03860
(603) 356-3666
www.moonscents.com

Edge of the Circle Books
701 E. Pike
Seattle, WA 98122
(206) 726-1999
www.edgeofthecircle.com

Ravens World
15600 NE 8th Street
Bellevue, WA 98008
(425) 644-7502
www.ravensworld.com

JBL Statues
Sacred Source/JBL
P.O. Box WW
Crozet, VA 22932-0163
(800) 290-6203
www.jblstatue.com

Pagan and Magical Journals and Magazines

New Moon Rising
P.O. Box 1731
Medford, OR 97501-0135
(541) 858-9404
www.nmrising.com

SageWoman
P.O. Box 641
Point Arena, CA 95468
(707) 882-2052
www.sagewoman.com

Shaman's Drum
P.O. Box 97
Ashland, OR 97520

Open Ways
P.O. Box 87704
Vancouver, WA 98687
www.9houses.org

Widdershins
Emerald City/Silver Moon Productions
12345 Lake City Way NE, Suite 268
Seattle, WA 98125
www.widdershins.org

Appendix Three—Chakra Chart

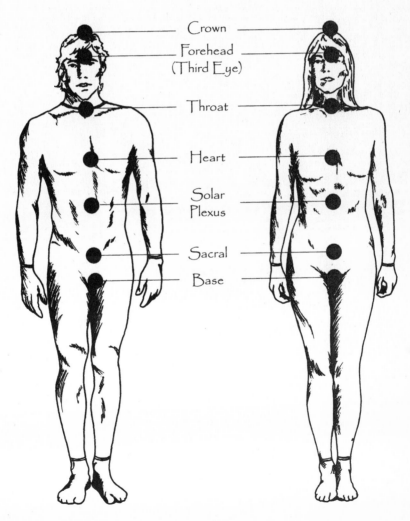

Crown

Forehead
(Third Eye)

Throat

Heart

Solar
Plexus

Sacral

Base

Glossary

A'a—A rough, chunky lava that flows thick and slow.

Annis—A cannibalistic Faerie hag, also called Black Annis.

Arcadia—A pleasant rural region of Greece.

Artemis—The Greek goddess of the Hunt.

Aspirge—To ceremonially cleanse by sprinkling with herbed or purified water.

Aura—The universal energy field surrounding all matter.

Bale fire—A ritual bonfire, traditionally held on Beltane.

Beltane—A Celtic fertility festival traditionally held May 1.

Brighid—Celtic goddess of fire, healing, poetry, and smithery.

Candlemas—A Christianized celebration of Imbolc.

Centering—The act of finding an internal point of balance.

Cerridwen—A Welch grain and moon goddess.

Chakra—One of the energy points located along the body.

Chakra, base—The energy point on the body associated with physical existence and the Kundalini force (see Kundalini).

Chakra, crown—The energy point on the body associated with our connection to universal energy.

Chakra, forehead—The energy point on the body associated with the third eye (our center of psychic awareness).

Chakra, heart—The energy point on the body associated with love, both personal and universal.

Chakra, sacral—The energy point on the body associated with sexuality and physical connections to others.

Chakra, solar plexus—The energy point on the body associated with emotional connections to others.

Chakra, throat—The energy point on the body associated with the ability to communicate with the self and others.

Cleansing—The act of removing negative vibrations or purifying.

Copse—A glen or grove of trees.

Corn dolly—A doll made of cornstalks representing the harvest.

Divine Marriage—The sacred mating of the God and Goddess (see *Hieros Gamos* and *Great Rite*).

Elementals—Beings that derive their essence from the various elements: earth, air, fire, water, ice, snow, and so on.

Elements—The elements that make up life: earth, air, fire, and water.

Eostre—The Saxon goddess of spring. Easter is named for her.

Equinox, Autumnal—The point during autumn when the sun crosses the celestial equator; day and night are of equal length (see *Mabon*).

Equinox, Spring—(see *Equinox, Vernal* and *Ostara*).

Equinox, Vernal—The point during spring when the sun crosses the celestial equator; day and night are of equal length (see *Ostara*).

Faerie—One of the denizens of the faerie kingdom or realm. A spirit or being connected with nature, usually with a specific plant or element.

Faerie sight—The ability to see into the faerie realm; the ability to see into other dimensions.

Grall—The drink Cerridwen made for her son that Gwion Bach drank by mistake.

Great Rite—The sexual union between Priest and Priestess, either symbolic or actual, representing the union of the God and Goddess (see *Hieros Gamos* and *Divine Marriage*).

Green Man—The divine male; the masculine aspect of nature.

Grounding—The act of rooting the self firmly in the physical world in preparation for magical or metaphysical work.

Guardian spirit—A spirit or energy being that protects or guards a person, place, or thing.

Guide—For this book, a person who leads others through guided meditations.

Guided meditation—(see *Meditation, guided*).

Gwion Bach—A servant of the goddess Cerridwen who later became her son Taliesin, the first Celtic bard (see *Taliesin*).

Hieros Gamos—The sacred moment when the God and Goddess come together in divine sexual union (see *Divine Marriage* and *Great Rite*).

Higher self—a person's total being. Also *inner self*.

Hina—A Hawaiian ancestral goddess connected with the moon, forests, and ocean.

Holly King—The aspect of the god who rules over the waning half of the year, from Litha to Yule; one of the origins of Santa Claus.

Hunt—The Wild Hunt led by various Gods and/or Goddesses.

Hunter—The Horned God of the Witches.

Imbolc—The celebration of the Goddess Brid traditionally held February 2.

Immolg—Literally, "in milk"; another version of Imbolc.

Kelpie—A Scottish water faerie who lures men to their deaths.

Kitska—A tool used in the art of *pysanky*.

Kundalini—The energy force of the body beginning at the base chakra and flowing up through the spinal column; associated with sexuality, psychic work, and vitality.

Lava—Molten rock that has reached the surface of the earth through a volcano or fissure; molten rock that has reached the surface of the earth and then hardened.

Litha—A festival honoring the Sun King and the Goddess in their prime (see *Solstice, Summer*).

Long pause—A thirty-second pause during a guided meditation.

Lugh—The Celtic god associated with the sun and harvest. Also called Lugh the Long Handed.

Lughnasadh—The Celtic festival of the god Lugh traditionally held August 1.

Mabon—A festival honoring the harvest (see *Equinox, Autumnal*).

Magic—The manipulation of natural forces and psychic energy to bring about desired changes.

Magma—Molten rock that has not yet reached the surface of the earth (see *Lava*).

Mandala—An intricate visual pattern used for meditation and focus in Hindu and Buddhist traditions. They are often symbolic of the universe.

Mantra—A word or combination of letters chanted over and over again. They are designed to bring one closer to divinity.

Meditation—A state of reflection and/or contemplation.

Meditation, guided—A mental journey through which one learns more about the self and/or through which one contemplates a predetermined concept.

Meditation, transcendental—(see *transcendental meditation*).

Midsummer's Eve—The night preceding the Summer Solstice.

Naiad—A Grecian water nymph or water faerie.

Nymph—A Grecian woodland spirit or forest faerie.

Oak King—The aspect of the god who rules over the waxing half of the year, from Yule to Litha.

Obsidian—Volcanic glass, usually lustrous and black.

O'helo—Hawaiian berries sacred to the goddess Pele.

Òhi'a lehua—A flowering Hawaiian tree associated with the goddess Pele.

Ostara—A festival celebrating the goddess Eostre (see *Equinox, Vernal*).

Pagan—A follower of Paganism.

Paganism—One of many ancient (and/or modern revivals of) Earth-centric and eco-centric religions.

Pahoehoe—A thin, easily flowing lava.

Pegasus—A Grecian winged horse.

Pele—The Hawaiian goddess of volcanoes and fire. She is the creatrix of the Hawaiian Islands chain. Contrary to popular belief, no one, virgin or otherwise, was ever sacrificed to the goddess by being tossed into the volcanoes. Human sacrifice in Hawai'i was reserved for the war god Ku.

Phoenix—The Egyptian bird that was consumed by fire every five hundred years and rose, renewed, from the ashes.

Puna—The southern section of the big island of Hawai'i.

Pysanky—The intricate art of Ukrainian egg decorating.

Sabbat—One of the eight Pagan holidays that comprise the Wheel of the Year.

Samhain—The Celtic festival of the dead traditionally held November 1.

Saturnalia—A seven-day Roman festival celebrating the god Saturn. Celebrated during the time of the Winter Solstice.

Short pause—A pause to a slow count of between five and seven during a guided meditation.

Sidhe (Daoine Sidhe)—Children of the Goddess Danu. Celtic faerie folk.

Smudge—The act of purifying with sacred smoke and/or incense.

Solstice, Summer—The point when the sun is at its zenith over the Tropic of Cancer, during the month of June. It is the longest day of the year (see *Litha*).

Solstice, Winter—The point when the sun is at its zenith over the Tropic of Capricorn, during the month of December. It is the shortest day of the year (see *Yule*).

Sun King—The lord of the sun (see *Oak King*) connected with the waxing half of the year.

Styx—The Grecian river over which the souls of the dead are ferried. It is a river of Hades.

Sylphs—The faerie spirits of the air.

Taliesin—The father of Celtic bards; he was originally Gwion Bach, servant of the goddess Cerridwen. Through a series of transformations (the last being his transformation into a grain of corn that Cerridwen, transformed into a hen, swallowed), Cerridwen became pregnant with Gwion and gave birth to his new form, Taliesin.

Totem animal—An animal spirit and/or essence connected to a human spirit and/or essence.

Trance—A state of altered consciousness. It is a hypnotic or ecstatic state of consciousness.

transcendental meditation—A specific form of meditation aimed at achieving deep emotional and physical relaxation, especially through the use of a mantra.

Tuonela—The Finnish realm of the dead.

Underworld—The realm of the spirit; the realm of the dead.

Undine—The faerie spirit of the water.

Unicorn—A magical horned horse.

Wicca—A modern revival of ancient Earth-centric religions focusing on the God and Goddess of Nature.

Wiccan—A practitioner of Wicca.

Will-o'-the-wisp—The faerie lights or energy beings that can and will lead humans astray in swamps, marshes, moors, and the forest.

Witch—A practitioner of the craft of magic.

Witchcraft—The art of magic.

Yule—A midwinter festival celebrating the rebirth of the Sun King (see *Solstice, Winter*).

Bibliography

Andrews, Ted. *Enchantment of the Faerie Realm*. St. Paul: Llewellyn, 1993.

Brennan, Barbara Ann. *Hands of Light*. New York: Bantam, 1988.

Cabot, Laurie. *Power of the Witch*. New York: Delacorte, 1989.

Campanelli, Pauline. *Ancient Ways*. St. Paul: Llewellyn, 1991.

Conway, D. J. *The Ancient and Shining Ones*. St. Paul: Llewellyn, 1993.

Cunningham, Scott. *Hawaiian Religion and Magic*. St. Paul: Llewellyn, 1994.

Encyclopedia Britannica.

Farrar, Janet and Stewart. *The Witches' Goddess: The Feminine Principle of Divinity*. Custer, WA: Phoenix, 1987.

———. *The Witches' God: The Masculine Principle of Divinity*. Custer, WA: Phoenix, 1989.

Frazier, Sir James George. *The Golden Bough*. New York: Criterion Books, Inc., 1959.

Froud, Brian, and Alan Lee. *Faeries*. New York: Bantam, 1978.

Galenorn, Yasmine. *Embracing the Moon*. St. Paul, MN: Llewellyn, 1998.

———. *Dancing with the Sun*. St. Paul, MN: Llewellyn, 1999.

———. *Crafting the Body Divine*. Santa Cruz, CA: The Crossing Press, 2001.

———. *Sexual Ecstasy and the Divine*. Berkeley, CA: The Crossing Press, 2003.

Kane, Herb Kawainui. *Pele, Goddess of Hawai'i's Volcanoes*. Captain Cook, Hawaii: Kawainui Press, 1987.

Mariechild, Diane. *Mother Wit: A Feminist Guide to Psychic Development.* The Crossing Press, Berkeley 1981.

Pennick, Nigel. *Practical Magic in the Northern Tradition.* Wellingborough, England: Aquarian Press, 1989.

Starhawk. *The Spiral Dance.* New York: Harper & Row, 1979.

Index